PRESS

940.
544

The Year in the Life of a Cowboy
by Owen D. Roane

Printed in the United States of America

ISBN 1-594670-64-1

Xulon Press
www.XulonPress.com

Xulon Press books are available in bookstores everywhere, and on the Web at www.XulonPress.com.

DEDICATION

I would like to dedicate this book to the many members of the 100th Bombardment Group who in a support role kept the group ready for action. They too suffered heartaches when the bombers failed to return from missions. I especially want to honor the maintenance people that worked countless hours to ensure the air crews the best chance possible to make it back to Thorpe Abbotts. They grieved as members of the team when they faced the loss of their comrades in the air. I am sure my own crew chief would share the honor bestowed on him by Major General E. E. Partridge, Commander of the Eighth Air Force's Third Air Division: "Master Sergeant Ray C. Morton has been awarded the Legion of Merit medal for exceptionally meritorious conduct in the performance of outstanding services as a crew chief of heavy bombardment aircraft from 29 June, 1943 to 13 May, 1944. Master Sergeant Morton, by his skill, leadership and untiring effort, has inspired his ground crew to an exceptional degree of efficiency. The efficiency and devotion to duty by Master Sergeant Morton has been a credit to himself and the Armed Forces of the United States." My crew and I wanted to express our personal thanks to Ray Morton and crew for the maintenance work that played such a large part in the completion of our tour of duty in the unfriendly skies over Europe, but such gratitude was too often unspoken at the time.

TABLE OF CONTENTS

PREFACE

M Y STARTING TO WRITE THIS RECORD of time with the 100th Bombardment Group was due in most part to the urging of my children. After completing a few chapters, my larger family voiced a desire to have copies of the end results. There were seven boys of my sibling group who served in various military units during World War II and the eldest was involved with the CCC as a supervisor. My mother and dad proudly displayed seven silver stars in the home window but, during the time covered in this writing, one of those stars was replaced with a gold one. All of my brothers have passed on without documentation of their service, so it is left to me to make record of their devotion to our country.

Their individual stories would take volumes to write and, since the information to do justice to such an undertaking is not readily available, I will tell my story in their honor. Perhaps, God willing, I will turn my thoughts and actions to family history writing with what future time is allowed.

I plan to include my crewmen and other friends that have knowledge of the "Bloody Hundredth" and have shown interest in my project, for distribution of copies of this book. This, of course, includes my friends in England that I have gotten to know through the efforts of the group that have spent endless hours and pounds to proudly show all visitors to Thorpe Abbots what our wartime unit did, through the establishing and maintaining of the museum. The great effort of my late friend Mike Harvey and all the numerous workers must have copies of this book for personal gifts as well as a desired amount to sell at the museum.

COWBOY ROANE, 1942

FLYING FORTRESS

SINCE THIS STORY HAS TO HAVE A BEGINNING, I believe it should start with my introduction to the faithful aircraft that I would spend one year with, learning to respect as well as depend on for my future security. My first flight day wasn't a very casual affair. We flew four hours and fifty-five minutes doing ten take-off and landing exercises with half being attempted by me. We picked up a navigator and flew two more hours for local orientation. We then had a leisurely thirty minute lunch and flew four hours and fifty minutes more of take-off and landing training. After our evening meal, we went for two hours of night flying. The foregoing episode in my life happened on the twenty-first day of November 1942, at Gowen Field, Boise, Idaho.

I had been assigned as co-pilot with an elderly man, probably in his late twenties named Richard C. King. He was a full fledged pilot with the rank of second lieutenant, a rank I couldn't even spell, much less be expected to hold intelligent conversation with someone of that lofty position. Our flight engineer was Staff Sergeant Trafford Curry, which rank I could spell, as I had that rank for a few hours just eleven days earlier to have it snatched away when I was elevated to Flight Officer. No one had heard of such a rank and no insignia to designate such a position was available. Actually, there were ten of us with new pilot wings to report at Gowen Field with gold bars and a band of blue scotch tape wrapped around the middle. We arrived with orders in hand that read as follows:

The following-named Flight Officers, Class 42-J, having completed the required course of instructions at the AAFAFS, Ellington Fld, Tex. are, under the provisions of AR95-60, WD, dd

Aug 20, 1942 and AAF Regulation 50-7, dd Sept 11, 1942, rated pilots eff Nov 10, 1942:

NAME	SERIAL NO.
BRINK, EUGENE	T120115
DAVIDSON, B. H. (IO)	T120122
RAY, WAYNE S.	T120179
ROANE, OWEN D.	T120216
TRAYLOR, EDWARD E.	T120203
HOPP, DONALD K.	T120146
NOXON, DONALD E.	T120172
RIDLEY, BILL B.	T120183
SWOPE, WESLEY H.	T120201
STEWART, LATIMER L.	T120196

No one questioned our strange rank or rating as warm bodies were the pressing need and, no doubt, we were "hot."

The twenty-second was devoted to getting acquainted and participating in ground training. The other members of the crew that I met were Lieutenant Ernest Anderson, navigator; Lieutenant Edward Hovde, bombardier; Staff Sergeant Rudolph Harmes, ball turret gunner; Staff Sergeant Barney Sutton, waist gunner; Staff Sergeant Heber Hogge, waist gunner; and Staff Sergeant Donald Wise, tail gunner. King conducted the get-acquainted session by telling us what he had done before the war. He then asked me what I had been doing, and I told of my training at Chanute Field as airplane mechanic, but decided to try for Sergeant Pilot when the opportunity came. He wanted to know what I had worked at before enlisting and I told him I had been a cowboy. Thus came the name, "Cowboy."

On the twenty-third, we flew nine hours and fifty minutes of transition training. We shared the airplane, a B-17E, with two other crews in training. We would often change crews with the engines running. Some airplanes were reported to have flown over twenty-five hours on a busy day. We finished our first phase training on the twenty-seventh with a total of thirty-one hours during our short stay at Gowen Field. After we completed our duty there, we made a trip to town that night to visit a place named "Buffalo Tavern" which was a must for Phase I indoctrination. We left early as we were catching a train the next morning for a place named Wendover Field, Utah.

We arrived at Wendover on the last day of November with the realization that all we had heard about the place was true. There were not towns of note within sight, which was considerable on a clear day. There was no security fence around the air base, and that unfamiliar situation was explained by "Nobody wants to get on this base and those trying to leave can be observed from the control tower for three days." According to the records of Jim Brown, assistant to Richard Le Strange in writing Century Bombers, "The training at Wendover turned out to be a rough grind for both air and ground personnel." Whenever possible, a practice mission was scheduled each day, with each mission averaging about five hours. We were fitted into that routine with bombing and air-to-ground gunnery, night flying and finally night navigation.

On the twenty-third of December, we climbed aboard our B-17F for an approximate five hour navigation training mission at 1800 local, which to non-military people means "when the night is beginning to lower," for a routine flight. We planned to return to Wendover about 2300 so were not prepared for a long, drawn out episode. Our flight was planned for a two-legged jaunt to St. George, Utah and return. When we located St. George, everything seemed to be going as planned. But when we turned back north toward Wendover, things changed. We flew into dense snow clouds, and our radio cut out on us. We climbed to 16,000 feet and

3

continued flying our planned heading. We could get nothing but static on the voice radio and our radio compass would do nothing but spin around. King told me to do the flying and he would keep vigil on the radio. The radio operator was instructed to attempt to reach our home station by short wave code and find out what the weather was like there. He received the requested report and checked out of the net. The word was that all Utah air fields were socked in due to a sudden, unexpected snow storm. Then the radio man was asked to seek advice as to where we were to go, but he couldn't raise the station or any other station again. Well, there we were on our own without definite location as we had been tooling around over where we imagined Wendover was located and had no reason to think the weather would give us a break before our fuel ran out.

We continued north hoping to break out and find an airport where we could land. I was getting tired of flying instruments while keeping a safe altitude and constant heading. I had only three hours of under the hood instrument flying in the B-17 and kept noticing my heading would drift off toward the east. Midnight came and I wished the crew Merry Christmas Eve, but most were too shaken to acknowledge the greeting. Our navigator, Anderson, kept trying to be of help, but nothing seemed to be working. We were lost and didn't know where we were going, but we were making good time. At this time we started following our emergency procedures and turned east to try to break out of the weather mass.

At 0200, we still had nothing to be cheerful about as we had neither seen nor heard anything to be of help. On occasion, we would turn on the landing lights to see nothing but snow flying toward us and we heard nothing but the drone of the engines pulled back as far as safety would permit in order to squeeze out all the time we could. Curry, the engineer, was watching fuel levels constantly to make sure all engines would have an equal supply. We began to plan our exit from the plane. We knew we were over mountains. It would be very dark and, of course, it would be very cold. We decided we would put the plane on automatic pilot and all jump simultaneously for combined help. At 0220 one engine quit so we feathered the prop, drained remaining drops of fuel and retrimmed the plane to fly on three. All were waiting for the order to jump but, with one final look, I saw a green rotating beacon like a star in the east. We turned the landing lights on and what to our wondering eyes should appear but two lovely rows of lights. King made radio contact as we lost another engine, luckily on the other side. We began a long glide past the airport and turned back to a final approach heading. King took over and called for gear down and twenty degrees of flaps. We touched down on the very first part of the runway and got on the brakes to come to a rapid stop near the other end. We turned around and a third engine stopped. We had to be towed to the terminal.

We were at Rock Springs, Wyoming on the most elevated commercial airport in the United States. King called Wendover to request instructions and we were told to remain there until aviation fuel could be trucked to us from Hill Field, Ogden, Utah. Hovde and King decided to stay with the plane as someone needed to be there to make decisions and guard the bombsight, besides they were both married and their wives were in Salt Lake City, Utah. I went in with the rest of the crew to a hotel for a few hours sleep. When word got around in Rock Springs, we were points of interest. Rock Springs was the first city in the United States to sell enough bonds to qualify in the "Buy a Bomber" campaign. We were interviewed and invited as guests of honor at a Christmas Eve dance at the Lions Club. Of course, civilians were invited to go to the airport and see a result of their bond buying. Christmas Day, after refueling, we made our departure in view of a much awed crowd. Of course we had just enough fuel to get to the base at Salt Lake City. Let this serve as a delayed correction to the account as told in the previously mentioned Century Bombers.

We completed our training at Wendover on December the thirty-first and without reluctance, boarded a train for Sioux City, Iowa for our final polish. However, due to sub-zero temperatures, we were not able to start flying again until the eighth of January. This gave us time to discover Sioux City, learn to pronounce the name and enjoy the hospitality. When we did start flying, we made up for lost time. By the end of January, we had amassed 168:10 hours of flying time in the B-17 and were ready to go over and fight the war. That was not to be at that time. For some reason the group was to be broken up, with flying crews scattered around the United States. Our crew and three others were sent to Walla Walla, Washington to assist training as instructor crews.

In early February, we received word that one of my classmates, Flight Officer Latimer Stewart, had been killed in a crash in Kansas with Paul Capaccio and three more men in his crew. A few days later, John Ray and eight of his crew flew into a mountain near Walla Walla. All of them were killed. The hazards of flying were becoming all too apparent.

My duties at Walla Walla can best be described as utility co-pilot. I did get to fly with some important people: Colonel Shorty Wheless, Captain Swah and other pilots wanting to take trips in government aircraft. While on one such trip we stopped to remain overnight in Boise, Idaho. I decided to call my girl back home who would, in two short months, be my wife. Betty, by name, asked me if I was going to be able to come home and I explained that the Air Corps was stingy with giving leave from duty at that time. About an hour later, I received a call from one of my brothers who was still at home, telling me of the death of my brother, Orville, in a B-26 aircraft crash, and that they were having a memorial service in Valley View, Texas. He had hopes my other brothers in the service and I could be there. Betty realized after talking with me that I probably had not been notified of the tragedy and called Lloyd, my brother still in the area.

Orville and I had both been in Class 42-J but were sent to different bases. He was co-pilot on a B-26 crew piloted by John

Bell Williams of Mississippi, another state in the union, of which he later became Governor. Williams was the sole survivor. We flew back to Walla Walla early the next morning. I got an emergency leave and Colonel Wheless flew me to Sioux City where I caught a train to Valley View in time to be there for the memorial service.

When I returned to Walla Walla I had accumulated 224 hours of B-17 pilot time. As luck would have it, there was an incident where the pilot of one of the crews of the Reed Provisional Group training there was removed from his crew, and his engineer, Staff Sergeant Robert Stuart had gone to the lock-up minus his stripes. Captain Swah called me up to see if I wanted to take the crew. I met with them and decided to have a go at it. The bombardier, Curtis Campbell, was another Texan in whom I could trust. Further, he had attained the wisdom that goes with age, twenty-eight at the time. He much later told me that he really doubted the wisdom of going into combat with a twenty year old pilot, but they hadn't been too keen on their previous pilot, and the co-pilot was from Oklahoma with some thirty hours in the plane, creating two strikes against him. I was told that I could have any unassigned engineer on the base to compete the crew. I couldn't find anything but rejects for the job so I asked Campbell about Private Robert Stuart and was given a thumbs up report on him. He was from Paducah, Kentucky and was a full-fledged airplane mechanic, also aged twenty-eight, and would be forever grateful to leave his current place of abode. I chose Stuart, a choice that served well in our being able to make twenty-five missions safely, so to speak.

The plane we were assigned was in the hangar getting a new wing tip, but it was repaired in time for our second phase training. At Curtis Campbell's suggestion we named it "Bigassbird" like the later "Sesame Street's" character without the middle name. Next thing, "Okie," the co-pilot, seemed unhappy with the now constituted crew so he was allowed to seek his fortune elsewhere. We got a new one, Arthur C. "Bud" Stipe, from Luke Field just out of flight school. He would play many parts in my life from that time onward.

For our final phase training we went to an auxiliary base at Madras, Oregon. Bud Stipe had been living at Bend, Oregon and knew many of the residents of the area. In fact, he had a wife in that vicinity. He brought a man out to meet us who was introduced as the mayor of Prineville, Oregon. We showed him around the "Bird" and I asked him if he would like to take a flight with us that day. He allowed that would be great, so our waist gunner, Sergeant Arthur Hauge, said he wasn't adverse to staying behind as we had planned mostly a navigation flight. Hauge's flying clothes fit His Honor very well, so off we went. On returning to the airfield, we flew over Prineville at 5,000 feet to give our guest a view of his hometown. He said he couldn't make out much from that vertical view, so we gave him a horizontal look at the subject. On landing, Captain Swah met us and said we must go directly back to Walla Walla as a report had been called to the Base Commander at Madras stating some B-17 with our name and number had flown extra low over Prineville. As soon as we had made the necessary crew change, we departed.

Of the crews of the Reed Provisional Group, there was only one that we got to know really well. That was crew 27-B with a pilot named John K. Justice. I hate to admit it but I used him rather badly on our trip overseas; however, I think he has finally forgiven me for causing him misery. We were getting ready to depart Walla Walla for Oklahoma City for final modification on our planes, and Colonel Reed came up to me and asked how the Big Bird was flying. Being of a suspicious nature, I shook my head and said that there was something strange about how she was acting, but I was sure Justice and some of the others were having good luck with their airplanes. Justice had the company of Colonel Reed until we arrived in England.

When we arrived at Tinker Field in Oklahoma, Colonel Reed met me at Operations with orders making me a Second Lieutenant and said I could have any of my enlisted men promoted to their provisional ranks. I said I would like to promote my engineer from private to technical sergeant, and he said it would be done. Further, there would be a week lay-over there and anyone wanting to go home could do so if I thought there would be no trouble getting them back. I stopped by the post exchange and bought some gold bars and a set of technical sergeant stripes. I called the crew together and gave them the news. I asked each one what they planned. Stipe said he couldn't make it to Oregon and back in that time limit, so I invited him to go home with me. The other two officers decided they could make it. Red Stuart said he didn't want to go home, as he had been a staff sergeant the last time he was home and didn't want to have to explain a slick sleeve. I gave him the chevrons I had bought and told him he could just explain that he had to make room for the new rank. It took some convincing to make him believe it was real. He then talked to the other sergeants of the crew, and convinced them that one hour late could spell their disaster. Red was quite a man and he was believable. Tomb, Jarvie and Healy were all three from Pennsylvania, so they headed back to the mines. I believe Stroble stayed at Tinker Field to make sure of the modifications on our plane.

Bud Stipe, Curtis Campbell, Dan Schmucker and I caught a bus heading south to Gainesville, Texas; Princeton, Texas; and New Orleans, Louisiana, as Schmucker, our navigator, was a product of New Orleans. I had failed to tell Bud that Betty and I were getting married and I wanted him to be my best man. The rest of the time he would be entertained by my brother Lloyd, who was waiting to join the Sea Bees.

Owen D. Roane

Roane

Stipe

Campbell

Schmucker

A Year in the Life of a Cowboy

On the twenty-sixth day of May, Curtis Campbell came by in his own car with his wife, Lois, and picked up Bud Stipe, Betty and me. We went to Tinker to find our Bird ready to go. We spent the night at the Skirvin Tower Hotel, said our good-byes early the next morning, and left the women to drive back to Texas. We flew to Smokey Hill Air Base at Celina, Kansas for a short course in instrument flying. I actually made our takeoff, flew a short cross country and returned to the field for landing under the hood. On the thirtieth, we started our trip to the European Theater of Operations. We stayed the next night at Selfridge Field, Michigan. Unfortunately, we never made it to Detroit as the city was in the throes of a race riot. On the first of June, we flew to Bangor, Maine by way of Niagara Falls. It was a shame Betty couldn't look at the falls with me, but Campbell still tells about the close-up view that the men in the nose of the plane were afforded.

The weather over the North Atlantic held us at Bangor another day and a crap game broke out. The third of June was used to make another short hop to Goose Bay, Labrador where the game continued. On the fourth we caught up to the weather where we made an instrument let down to land on the tarmac at Bluie West 2, Greenland. We were briefed that we must fly up the fjord, whatever that was, and land on the first try, as the walls of the fjord were too close together to make a turn around. They didn't however tell us what to do if by chance there floated a large iceberg at the landing end of the runway. It turned out that they were wrong about the narrowness of the gorge.

We had to hold up another day in Greenland so we made a hike on the tundra, shot a ptarmigan and enjoyed the Arctic scenery. On the sixth, we were again allowed to make another leg of our journey, this leg to Iceland. Three things I remember about Iceland were: the mess hall closed while it was still broad daylight, a terribly smelly latrine where Kilroy had been, and Schmucker taking all the money I had won up until that time. He cleaned me of $280.00 in about twenty minutes. We went to town and ate dinner at the Jorg Hotel in Reykjavik where the local people were eating with their fork in their left hand, but we never said anything, as we didn't want to embarrass them. We went fishing off the dock where we caught some fish that were nearly all head; Lion fish I think they called them. Needless to say, we didn't worry about not being able to eat them.

On the tenth of June, we continued our journey; however, we caught up with all that nasty weather that had preceded us and we started having the usual radio compass trouble while still far away from our first checkpoint, Stornoway, Scotland. Schmucker wanted me to make a correction to the left, but I was still mad at him and refused to comply. He insisted once more on a left turn, but knowing somewhat about geography, I realized that an error that direction could lead us to Norway, and we knew that would be a waste of aircraft and crew if we ended up there. After what seemed like several weeks, I heard a faint "da dit" on the radio compass. The homing device showed us nothing, but I knew there would eventually be a beam we could bracket. The Good Lord finally took over and let us find Prestwick, Scotland. I am afraid I gloated some to our navigator. On the twelfth of June, we flew to some place in England identified as L.S.. I thought it meant Lost Squadron. At any rate, we had our aircraft required of us there but I will not go into the details of what became of the "Bigassbird."

We left that same day to go to Bovingdon to attend an ETO familiarization course conducted by members of the RAF. We were brought down to earth by learning that the German ME-109 and FW-190 fighter aircraft could out-fly the B-17 at 30,000 feet altitude. They taught us about counter measures called "Window," about "Darkey," the audio messenger on the ground that could give us a heading to our station, and how to determine by the wailing sound in our radios whether we were approaching barrage balloons or moving away from them. All the subjects were valuable for our success in flying around England.

The second day at Bovingdon there was no school, so Campbell, Stipe, Schmucker and I went to London to see the sights. A very friendly cab driver took us on a tour of the city. There we saw all the bombed out areas of the town, the normal tourist attractions, and he showed us where the Red Cross Clubs were located. He warned us of the hazards of Piccadilly Circus and showed us the "tube" entrances where we could find safety from bombs. Our fee for the trip was only one pound Sterling each, which wasn't bad at all.

At Bovingdon, we were billeted with three other crews. Justice and I were from the Reed Group and the other two were from the Sanders Group, which also just arrived in England. Henington, a pilot from Houston, Texas and Moreno, from Fillmore, California headed the other crews. The sixteen officers from the crews were usually shooting pool and discussing how to win the war. The other pilots didn't have first hand information about any groups, so they were interested in what I could tell them about the 100th Group. I related to them about the accomplished pilots that I personally knew from training with the 351st Squadron. We all four requested assignment to the 100th Bombardment Group, which just happened to have room for us on their roster. We were all trucked to Thorpe Abbotts to settle into our new home on the twenty-sixth of June. Justice, Henington, and I were assigned to the 349th Squadron, and Moreno to the 418th.

The following morning, we went to the 351st Squadron area and I introduced our crew to King's crew and Glenn Dye's crew. Dye had a co-pilot named Luckadoo. That name reminded me of a song I had heard.

Owen D. Roane

THE FIRST MISSION

JUNE THE TWENTY-SEVENTH, 1943 was settling in day. We signed for our combat supplies which included an escape and evasion kit loaded with French money. That was the prettiest money I had ever seen. Rembrandt himself must have done the artwork. There were two very intricate maps of France and Germany done on silk. We had our pictures made, dressed in some European peasant clothes, to be included in the kit just in case we should find ourselves afoot on the continent and in need of a passport. The most useful items we were issued that day were two English style bicycles. They were, of course, assigned to the pilot and co-pilot in order that we could coordinate maintenance work on our aircraft out on the hard stand. This issue brought up the hackles on the collective necks of Campbell and Schmucker. When things were explained to their near satisfaction (they were informed that bicycles could be bought in nearby Bungay and the supply truck would drive them over to the spot), they were somewhat mollified. Stipe and I agreed to take our bikes and go along with them to assist in getting their purchases back to base. They were not accomplished bike riders, so that was the least we could do.

We arrived in Bungay, and Curtis and Dan made their transactions. To the best of my memory, the selling price was ten pounds Sterling, and there were no problems in selection as there was only one style, color and price at that market. That seemed true for the whole of England. Dan and Curtis tried their luck riding, which was all bad, just as if the supply people knew that navigators and bombardiers hadn't the required coordination to ride bicycles or else they wouldn't have washed out of pilot training. After a few spills, it became obvious some further planning was necessary. Now in that small village there just happened to be a tavern across the street that needed reconnoitering. Stipe and I agreed to trail their bikes back to Thorpe Abbotts while they could catch a ride back or trot along behind us on the return trip, if they stood for the refreshments in that handy dispensing facility. After showing them our competence at riding one and trailing one, they acquiesced. What other choice did they have?

We enjoyed the local pub for some time, but the short night was descending and we needed to start home. Bud's riding skill and mine had diminished somewhat for our trip home. Again our erstwhile friends became discontented, and they started a vocal protest about the disgusting situation. They didn't relish the thought of walking and pushing five miles back when other contractual arrangements had been agreed upon. What was left of the day was saved when two Military Policemen came along in a weapons carrier. On learning the details of the distressful situation, they suggested they haul all of us and our bicycles back to the Thorpe Abbotts base as broken bones or other such encumbrances would not contribute positively to our carrying out our assigned duties toward the war effort.

When we arrived back at our squadron area, Campbell and Schmucker were still disconcerted about the payment in kind they had made for services not rendered. Stipe explained that their bicycles were safely home, and they had been privileged to ride that five miles instead of trotting along behind in the dark. I am sure they didn't completely accept the way the episode was resolved because, as a matter of fact, I still hear words of chastisement from Curtis Campbell regarding that event whenever he and I have the occasion to meet and relive days of our lives long ago. It shouldn't have mattered all that much because the first time we rode those things to the club, we no longer had possession of the same bicycles. Then we remembered that we had heard the Officers Club referred to as the local bike exchange.

On the thirtieth of June, after checking with the Squadron Commander for our interview, Captain Veal had us go up for an orientation flight with Sammy Barr who was Squadron Operations Officer. On the ensuing proficiency check, we were shown the area including some major checkpoints. The most notable point was a large balloon hangar at Pulham that was always a welcomed sight in days to come as it seemed to announce to us that one more mission was successfully chalked up to our account. Due to our base location it rivaled the White Cliffs of Dover for a most welcomed sight. Just after we landed, Captain Veal met us to get a report on our crew capabilities as replacements were sorely needed after the first mission where the 349th Squadron had lost three crews. Barr gave us a thumbs up and during the critique they were pleased to learn that I had accumulated more than four hundred hours flying time in the B-17. Captain Veal told us that we were to be assigned his airplane, "Laden Maiden," so named because of his wife's condition when he departed the United States.

We were driven out to our airplane dispersal area which had become vacant just five days earlier after the fateful raid on Bremen, Germany. We met Ray Morton and the rest of the ground crew of the "Laden Maiden." We especially wanted to get to know and become good friends with those men, because we realized our hoped for successful tour would depend, in large part, on their work and concern. Stuart told me that we had drawn a good crew chief after he and Ray did an extensive walk around the airplane. Ray learned from Stu that I was a Texan and he called a long tall individual over introduced him as a fellow Texan who would be helping to look after our plane as he was a member of the 349th Aircraft Inspection Unit. This man, Pete Cook, said he was from Saint Jo, Texas, which was one of Valley View's rivals in interscholastic competition. He mentioned knowing a fellow named Lloyd Roane from Gainesville, Texas and asked me if I knew him. I replied that I thought that he was one of my distant brothers from a family of nine boys. Pete would later enter into a conspiracy with Ray Morton that might have been instrumental in saving my life. They placed bulletproof glass in the side windows of the "Maiden" even though I had said that I didn't think the extra weight would be justified. The next mission proved me wrong as chips of glass fell in my lap from thirty caliber machine gun splatters in the cockpit window next to my head. A letter from Ray fifty years later on the occasion of Betty and I celebrating our Golden Wedding Day tells his concerns.

1943----1993

Dear Betty and Owen,

Congratulations on your 50th Wedding Anniversary – a special day for two special people, a day for celebrating. Sorry Thelma and I can't be with you to share your happiness on this Golden Anniversary.

I have reached that particular age when one begins to look wistfully at the remembrances of years past. I recall my first meeting with you, Cowboy – another 50th anniversary. It was 1943, the USA was at war with Germany, and I was stationed at a B-17 airbase in Thorpe Abbotts, England. As a ground Crew Chief, I had been assigned a ground crew and a new B-17 that had just been ferried over from the states. Our job was to have that plane readied for take-off when the call came down for a combat mission. When the air crew arrived for that first flight, I watched them climb aboard and I recall thinking; "Surely that young kid is not going to fly that plane." That young kid was you and the rest is history. You flew mission after mission with the "Laden Maiden" until a slight landing mishap, after a practice flight, grounded the plane. You were assigned a new plane, "The Bigassbird II." My crew and I stayed on to crew the new plane; the "Laden Maiden" was reassigned to another ground crew for repairing.

There was a special bond between that first air crew and my crew. I found myself being possessive to the point of nearly being "busted" for refusing anyone, other than you, to take the plane up. You completed your missions with "The Bigassbird II" and our paths never crossed again until forty-three years later when I attended my first 100th Bomb Group Reunion in Long Beach, California. It was there that I had the privilege of meeting you, Betty. I can understand why Cowboy was so "hell-bent" (Webster's definition reads: 'firmly resolved or recklessly determined') to complete those missions and return home to his young bride!

Thelma and I send our best wishes for years of continued love, health, and happiness. We treasure your friendship.

A life-long friend,
Ray Morton

Captain Veal wanted me to ride as observer on a combat mission with one of the seasoned pilots and his crew. There was an alert that night, and we were briefed very early next morning for a raid on a place on the coast of France named La Pallice. I was to make the trip with Victor Reed, not to be confused with Colonel Reed, our erstwhile Commander who flew over to England in the company of John Justice. I was to ride behind the co-pilot with standing room only. That was the location of the most appropriate alternative oxygen station. I could stoop down and just see out the front windshield. Needless to say, I was not unduly impressed with any part of the situation; however, due to adverse weather, we turned around short of the French coast, and I pondered the chance that I might not have to go through that "Baptism by Fire" after all.

After debriefing, Captain Veal met us with three important bits of information. I wouldn't have to go with another crew before going on missions, we had a new Group Commander named Neil B. Harding, and a message had arrived revoking my commission as a second lieutenant as I had failed to sign an oath of office before I departed Walla Walla, Washington. Once again, I was the lowest ranking officer on the crew, although I was the aircraft commander.

July Fourth came very early in the morning, and once more the Hundredth Bomb Group was briefed for a trip to La Pallice for a go at the submarine pens located there. Our crew was scheduled as the last alternate, but we actually were loaded with real live bombs. We were the first replacement crew to be alerted for a combat mission. If there were no vacant spots in the formation by the time we came abreast of the Brest Peninsula, we were to turn around and retrace our route home. Colonel Harding was flying command in the lead ship with Captain Turner, Commanding Officer of the 351st Bomb Squadron. That was the squadron I used to fly co-pilot for Richard King with Major Jack Kidd as Commanding Officer; however, he was now Lieutenant Colonel Kidd, Group Operations Officer. We took off and flew along in trail with one other airplane from the 349th Squadron for what seemed like days. Finally, one of the planes from the group turned back, and our companion crew pulled up to fill that slot. We continued trailing past Lizard Point over a great expanse of water. Schmucker explained that now was a period of our flight where our "Mae West" preservers could possibly become a welcomed part of our equipment instead of just additional baggage. Joe Stroble allowed that it had always made him feel more snugly packed into the ball turret.

Somewhat later, Schmucker announced that we were at our "go, no go" point, and we best turn back as it seemed that we were not going to be needed by the group. However, Stipe noted that the 95th Group just to our right and above us had a vacant spot in their low squadron. An opinion poll was taken over the interphone, and everyone said we would grasp the opportunity and go all the way. We were already five hours into the mission and it would be a shame not to get sortie credit for our effort. Unknown to us at this time, we were building on a record of always completing the mission any time we made a takeoff.

We joined the 95th Group and continued our trip. At a later date such a procedure involving another group was prohibited as it seems there were some B-17's tagging along with alien crew members. The practice of forming composite groups, however, continued with rendezvous being accomplished over England.

Before the target and before landfall, Stipe and I ran through our cruise checklist again and all gauges read within the proper ranges. A quick glance showed fuel level to be appropriate.

We began to see puffs of black smoke up ahead and saw a B-17 in trouble. Curtis Campbell at debriefing reported, "Way down low I observed one lone fighter heading back toward Paris, then I noticed one lone white circle way down below which seemed to be drifting opposite our direction of flight. Glancing back, I saw two more white blossoms. Wow! Rigor Mortis began to set in as I observed three men dangling below those blossoms. Those were parachutes and men bailing out! Stark Fright overwhelmed me as I suddenly realized those people were shooting at us."

We opened bomb bay doors with the rest of the 95th Group and toggled our bombs when the leader dropped his. With a feeling of relief and with a heavy load removed from our minds and plane, we headed back out to sea. That relative tranquility did not last long as we had number two engine sputter and die. For no reason we could comprehend, it just quit. On rechecking the fuel level gauge, it showed full. We were able to keep up with the group by advancing the throttles. The fuel gauge of the B-17 is a single multipurpose instrument. It had a rotating knob selector for checking individual tank measurements, although we kept the selector set on the number three engine main tank. Bud Stipe reached down and started rotating the selector to the other engine main tanks which revealed red fuel warning lights on all other positions. Stuart immediately started transferring fuel from the wing tanks into the mains although I had failed to retard the throttle, nor had I turned off the ignition on the dead engine. Thus when the fuel hit number two, it really came back to life giving us a surge within the formation of our adopted group.

The Good Lord saw me through once again although many things could have happened due to the malfunctioning fuel gauge and our failure to execute proper engine out check list. We could easily have had a runaway engine, could have thrown a propeller into the formation or we could have collided with another aircraft. Very tenuously we flew with the 95th to a point near their home base of Horham where we left in time to join the 100th Group for landing. Most of the crew didn't realize the peril we came through and we didn't make them aware of the episode. One mission under our belt and we were happy to be returning to "Grandpop," the code name for our station. Of course when Morton heard of the "Laden Maiden" fuel gauge malfunction, he got busy and changed it forthwith.

At debriefing, we learned that twenty-five planes from the Hundredth made the trip to La Pallice, but one crew with pilot Robert Pearson failed to come back. When they were last seen, they were heading south from the target with bomb bay doors open and were descending rapidly. It was reported by an observer that both inboard engines failed simultaneously and the crew bailed out. Could they also have had fuel gauge or fuel transfer trouble?

LE BOURGET

JULY FIFTH CAME AS A DAY OF REST because the English weather didn't allow for any mission attempt. We used the day locating the facilities most necessary for our duty and pleasure. Stipe and I had business at the link trainer building, and we later went by the aerial gunnery school. Our men were there discussing with the gunnery officer, Lieutenant Peter Theodore, about the value of tracer bullets comprising part of the loading of the fifty caliber ammunition belt. At the time, every fifth round was a tracer with two armour piercing and two incendiary cartridges between. The argument was whether or not the tracers followed the same trajectory as the other rounds in the belt and, if not, might it lead gunners to shoot behind and above the target? Our men wanted to keep the loading as it was because of the assurance the tracers gave them as well as an unnerving effect it might have on the enemy fighter pilots. Further, tracer tracks serve to alert gunners from other bomber crews of the fact there are unwelcome planes in our area. I gave my opinion in support of the crew, and the gunnery officer asked me what position I manned. I explained that I was the pilot, whereas he asked me why I did not wear my rank on my flying suit. I replied that there was no insignia around for my rank, and wouldn't be recognized if such was available. I was still smarting from being returned to Flight Officer status without a chance for promotion from that lowly station. He acknowledged sympathy for my plight, and we became friends afterward. As far as I know, the tracer use was continued.

On the sixth and seventh we gathered with other members of the group and flew practice missions, because a huge weather mass was still settled in over the continent. Colonel LeMay had indicated he approved of all groups in his division spending available hours engaging in such worthy training activities, because it would do us good. On the evening of the ninth we were alerted for a trip the following morning. At briefing we learned that our target was Le Bourget Air Field in Paris, France. I remembered that my greatest hero when I was a youth had been Charles A. Lindbergh, and I knew he landed his "Spirit of St. Louis" at that very field after he flew across the Atlantic Ocean. I was also aware that he was advanced in rank from first lieutenant to lieutenant colonel because of his heroic deed. Perhaps I could move from flight officer into his vacated rank by dropping bombs there, as Lindy had seemingly fallen into disfavor.

We made our takeoff and assembly according to plan and headed out across the English Channel. The Channel was wider than I had imagined from looking at maps; however, being our first direct crossing into enemy territory, we didn't mind the distance. Time was needed to check the guns and get ready for action and, in that respect, we were soon to see more than we had ever expected. We weren't crossing at the shortest point, Dover to Calais, but from Brighton to Dieppe. On our return from Paris we were to learn just how wide the Channel could be with Messerschmitts hounding us, and headwinds holding us back. The flight time across could be as much as ninety minutes, according to the prevailing westerly winds.

We had reached the outskirts of Paris when the mission was canceled due to the persistent cloud cover of the assigned target. When we turned to make our way back to the home base, it seemed that the Luftwaffe Flying School had let out and the whole student body had come out to play. We soon learned they were joined by their teachers in the activities. According to our late historian, Jim Brown, "The wing ran into the heaviest fighter opposition it had seen thus far." With the wind now in our face, we felt much like a person might feel while trying to escape across a very muddy field while a swarm of highly agitated bees was in hot pursuit. Furthermore, we didn't see hide nor hair of a promised Polish

Squadron and their Spitfires to give us much needed withdrawal support.

We saw one of our planes going down with two engines and a wing on the same side blazing. Ten chutes were counted over Dieppe, but the west winds were pushing them back over France. We learned later that the plane belonged to the Charles Duncan crew. During this battle, Pat Healy bagged an Me-109 from his tail position. Our men had managed to expend practically all the fifty caliber ammunition we had taken. After the attacks stopped and we were nearing England, Healy called from the tail gun position with a classic remark, "Boy, am I hungry." That remark was repeated as we neared the home base on all our future highly contested bomb deliveries.

On the twelfth of July we were still waiting for the weather to break over the continent. To keep from getting bored we were invited by Lieutenant Jack Herlihy, our squadron engineering officer, to take a B-17 that had recently undergone an engine change for a slow time flight. New engines needed to be pampered by slowly bringing them back into flight readiness. We invited any and all ground personnel who could spare the time and obtain a parachute to go fly with us. We were soon loaded and airborne, and the low flight over England was a good way to enjoy a grand view of the island we were making our temporary home. The flight was a small offering to the men who spent so many long hours keeping the airplanes ready to go, as well as the men who brought our supplies and munitions out to our planes. All went well in the flight that morning, and when we landed we learned that another airplane and another load of sightseers were lined up for us as an afternoon jaunt, if we were so inclined. We were happy to do as requested because such an unopposed leisurely flight was enjoyable to our crew as well as our passengers. At most reunions of the Hundredth Bomb Group Association I visited with men who flew with me on some of those slow time flights, and they really appreciated the thoughtfulness of our crew.

The following day, we went for another try at Le Bourget, but after boring holes in the sky over England for nearly four hours, we were recalled. We didn't get attacked that day, but we didn't get credit for a mission either. However, on the next day, July the fourteenth, we went there again with Colonel Harding leading. I thought the weather wouldn't dare be uncooperative this time, but by now the meteorological disturbances were being recognized as an enemy. Twenty-two planes left our station that day, but ten returned with varying excuses. Some pilots claimed aircraft malfunctions and others said they couldn't find the formation.

The story continues with twelve of us reaching the target, but only four dropped their bombs. I believe we were one of those four, and Campbell says we had our bombs fall on some sort of industrial plant on the opposite side of the Seine River from the Eiffel Tower. The bombardier of the group lead couldn't find the target and the other members of his squadron were supposed to drop on his release so they all took their bombs away. Our element leader did drop and we followed suit.

Again, the way home was not easy. Eight of our twelve planes sustained battle damage, including our own "Laden Maiden" as was pointed out by Pete Cook, our trusted aircraft inspector, when we returned to our revetment. Colonel Harding was not amused by the overall showing of the 100th Bomb Group, but we did get credit for another hard earned combat sortie to go along with our combat damage that we flaunted like a "Red Badge of Courage."

On the sixteenth, we were scheduled for another formation training flight. I taxied out behind Woodrow Barnhill and crew six of the 349th Squadron and started my takeoff run just as he was breaking ground. On his climb he went into a sharp right bank and slid off into the ground right under our flight path. We continued for a three hour flight with the image of black smoke from the explosion of Barnhill's plane crowding our minds. We didn't see how there could possibly be any survivors of the crash; however, after we landed, we learned that three men from the tail section were alive though gravely injured. The rest of the crew were dead. Carl Hudson, the co-pilot, walked away from the plane and explained how the accident happened, bummed a cigarette, sat down with his back to a tree and died. Stuart said, "See there Cowboy, that's what I've been telling you about those steep turns." I spent a lot of time trying to explain the difference between takeoff and landing for the likelihood of stalling out on turns, but I don't think he was persuaded so I suppose I did tone down my turn on final approach from then on.

The next day we went for a mission to Hamburg, Germany to try to destroy an aircraft engine plant. By now we were eager to bomb any industrial plant that supported the construction of Luftwaffe fighters. Once again we had to abandon the mission just short of the target as the weather failed to cooperate; however, our formation didn't go unnoticed as we were engaged by swarms of fighters. We were getting frustrated by having long costly battles with the German defense elements and still having no chance to drop our bombs on any vital installations. From the ensuing battle we suffered more battle damage to the "Laden Maiden," but after returning to our base we could exhibit four bombs and two swastikas painted on her nose, showing four missions and two enemy fighters to our credit. We spent time the next three days flying locally while the men of brass were contemplating the weather and our future targets.

Captain Veal called me in during this lax time and explained that his request for my promotion to first lieutenant had returned with a short notation that all flight officers must in the future appear in London before a promotion board of the Eighth Air Force. They would be considered for a direct commission if they were found deserving. Then, as a second lieutenant, they could be considered for promotion to first lieutenant after thirty days. The next such board would be meeting soon for which I could be scheduled to make my audition. I pondered the proposition and came to the conclusion that it would have been much simpler and more rewarding for me if the unknown administrative officer back in Walla Walla, Washington had just sent a TWX requesting that I execute an "Oath of Office" and keep my original commission.

The day of the scheduled promotion board came and I left early for the appointment. My bad luck, career wise, was holding true to form. The train was delayed due to damage done to the track by German bombing the previous night. When I arrived at the appointed place, the board meeting had concluded and no one was there except the Duty Officer. He had the records of the meeting, and sure enough, my name was on the list with five other Flight Officers. All the others had been approved for commissions. The Duty Officer was a warrant officer junior grade, and he must have felt my pain because he marked "approved" by my name and told me goodbye. I am not sure of the date of the incident but I was doubting the results, as my commission didn't come through until October.

BLITZ WEEK

ON THE EIGHTEENTH OF JULY we were alerted for a mission to Kassel, a target far inside Germany and, of course, it would be beyond the range of our friendly fighters. Just before the flight was to take off, it was canceled due to reports of poor weather lingering over the continent. To keep the crews from being too disappointed about not having a fllight to accomplish, our ever caring operations people scheduled a training flight. The following day, part of our crew flew a test hop on one of the group planes just out of major maintenance. I took the crew chief along on the flight as co-pilot to see for himself how the plane checked out. Shortly after takeoff, I realized enough attention had not been paid to the checklist. When I started my usual left turn, I encountered resistance to the movement. I then noticed that the aileron lock was still in place so rudder control was used to make the turn. After a safe altitude was attained, I noted the problem to my crew chief co-pilot as I banked the plane and removed the obstacle. I handed the locking pin to my helper for the day, and he made as if to throw it out the window. I have forgotten the individual's name, but I bet he hasn't forgotten the incident.

On the twenty-third, the meteorologist predicted that the huge low pressure area that had lingered over Northwest Europe for the last three months was giving way to a high. We figured if the forecast held we would be busy for the next few days going out to meet the Hun. Actually the briefing the next morning showed something very different on the agenda. Because our Wing, 402 C.B.W., had been equipped with extra wing tip fuel tanks, referred to as "Tokyo Tanks," we were selected to make a trip of 1900 miles to Trondheim, Norway with little opposition expected from German defenses. To obtain maximum fuel economy, we crossed

29

the North Sea and Norwegian Sea at 2,500 feet and climbed to 20,000 feet just before land fall to bomb submarine pens in the fjords 360 miles north of the Arctic Circle.

In all we had forty-one planes, including twenty-one from the 95th Bomb Group stationed at Horham, only five miles from Thorpe Abbotts. We dropped our 500 pound bombs on the target with only meager opposition from fighters and flak; however, Laden Maiden did sustain some damage to one wing and one plane made a crash landing in Northern Scotland. The lost plane belonged to Curtis Biddick. Two men on other 100th Bomb Group crews were wounded on the mission. Our flying time for that trip was twelve hours and twenty-five minutes. The Flying Fortress groups based to our north but having shorter range bombed over U-Boat pens in the southern part of Norway. Those groups were designated the First Bomb Division. We became the Third Bomb Division.

When our flying boots had barely stopped rocking from removal for retiring we were awakened to join our friends for briefing. At that gathering we learned of a maximum effort by bombers of the RAF to literally remove the city of Hamburg, Germany from the World War II competition. They had struck in force that night and were, even as the briefing officer spoke, returning to England. They had created mass confusion in Hamburg, not only from the area bombing but from a bomber aircraft defensive effort called Window. It was the dropping of millions of strips of tinfoil that caused false reflections on the German radar screens and rendered them useless. We were to join the RAF effort by daylight bombing for the next four days, while they continued their night raids. With much satisfaction, I thought of the Luftwaffe blitz of London.

The long range capability of our division aircraft dictated that we fly beyond Hamburg to Warnemunde to bomb an aircraft industry plant and also act as a diversion to the Luftwaffe to keep them from all swarming on Hamburg. Finding the primary target still covered by clouds, our Air Boss took us to Kiel to unload on our secondary target. The flak was intense and much heavier than the 88mm stuff that usually hammered us. The bursts were much larger, blacker, and louder. The plane from the 350th squadron being flown by Richard Carey in place of the ailing regular pilot, William DeSanders, was caught by a burst and was rapidly descending toward the Selenter Sea. I witnessed another scene where a large burst of flak caught a fort from another group just under the right wing. It broke the wing off, leaving the plane and crew to go into a dive toward the earth with no parachutes being counted. Laden Maiden would need much patchwork that night but the engines were sound and for our record, mission number six had been accomplished.

On the twenty-sixth, we departed for Hanover with Colonel Harding as Air Boss because we were leading our wing. We were to rendezvous over the Frisian Islands but the other groups didn't show. We had to either abort or go on into Germany alone, which we weren't too keen on doing, when our lead spotted a convoy off the coast of Germany. Since no friendly vessels should be there, we had a go at it, and several bombs hit among them. A new radio beacon called a splasher installed on the ground in East Anglia to help with wing assembly didn't help that day. But one more mission chalked up with no battle damage to our plane, and apparently we could sleep late next morning.

July twenty-eighth was another mission day, but our crew and the Laden Maiden were left off the alert listing. I didn't ever question the selection of crews for participation as I believed the operations people knew their business and I was not one to tempt fate by trying to pick the missions we would participate in. The formation returned early as weather again obscured the target and our group leader decided to turn back when the German coast was reached. They did experience a new defense system employed by the Luftwaffe that was concluded to be an attempt at air to air rocketry. Luckily the attempt failed to accomplish the heart's desire of the German Air Defense.

We gathered later that day in Class A uniform to receive our first Air Medals awarded for five bomber missions over enemy occupied territory. Now the challenge would be to get through the next fifteen missions to receive the three succeeding Oak Leaf Clusters to accompany the Air Medal. After that, to accomplish five more missions for a Distinguished Flying Cross and ticket home.

The following day we were alerted for the Warnemunde target that weather denied us just four days earlier. The flight in was made above a very substantial cloud deck. I was wondering if we were on the right track as only a few fighters and meager flak were dogging us. When we arrived at the target area, the target was clear, a quick run was made and bombs unloaded. We were told that it was a good strike.

The last two days of July we stayed on the ground and recounted the happenings of the first month in combat. We had logged ninety-one hours and fifty minutes aloft. We had credit for eight combat sorties but the group had lost three more planes and crews to enemy action. We had flown four missions in six days during the final part of July.

August the second came with a practice mission on the menu. We bored holes for four hours and on landing, an uneventful flight became eventful. We landed safely, but near the end of our landing roll, the airplane started acting up and went down on her knee on the left side. I let the airplane ground loop and ended up in the grass with the left wing down and one and two engines smoking. Campbell decided the best way out was through the astrodome. Schmucker meanwhile saw the engines smoking, grabbed the fire extinguisher, and pulled the CO2 activator. The resulting spray had nowhere to go but out through the astrodome. That relief valve was filled by Campbell scrambling out. The result was a stream of foam hitting Campbell in the seat as he was making his exit. He said that it was amazing how cold CO_2 was even through his flying clothes. The cause for the collapse wasn't pondered too long as we had no need to wonder why, we were only meant to continue to fly.

The ninth was a day to try to forget but fifty years have done little to dim the vision. Our plane was still in the docks and we were to practice formation flying. Sammy Barr offered his plane for my crew's use. I would have declined the offer of Torchy, but since Sammy was Operations Officer, I had not much choice. The plane was on hardstand number twenty, which was part of a combination of four parking places. Reeder was in number twenty-one parking place and was to lead our element on the flight. We had started Torchy and done our preliminary warm up but had to wait for Reeder to taxi past. A man on the ground just beyond my number one engine propeller was looking up at me as if he had something to say. I motioned toward Reeder's plane taxiing out but instead of turning to look, he backed up. The prop of Reeder's number four engine caught his head. And part of it-along with his cap-was tossed toward us. He dropped like an empty sack. We taxied out behind Reeder and flew our six hour flight silently as if none of us saw the catastrophe. On return, we learned the name of the victim. It was written out as Eldridge, Shirley B.

On August the tenth, the 100th Bomb Group took off on what was to have been the "Big Mission" but our crew was left behind to do a slow-time flight with Laden Maiden. The aircraft checked out fine as we knew it would. The maintenance people had replaced engines number one and two along with the left wing and landing gear. The group returned without making the briefed trip but with tight lips as the same mission would be flown later. Maybe the 100th formation would include us.

The twelfth of August was a mission day for the group but again, our crew was not included. Their bombs were dropped on Bonn causing considerable damage according to the photos. Victor Reed, with whom I was to have flown my first mission, had his airplane hit by flak over the target and one fragment penetrated his outer clothing but struck the silver wings he was always wont to wear. This episode so upset Reed that he was unable to fly any more missions. Also, the August twelfth mission flown by my friend, Glenn Dye, and his crew was their fifteenth straight mission which coincided with the fifteenth mission of the group.

On the fourteenth, we were called on to participate with the group in a decoy flight just off the coast of Belgium to attempt to bring the Luftwaffe out within range of our short range allied fighters. I never heard any report of the success of the scheme. No bombs, no enemy fighters, no flak, no damage and no mission credit. Nothing risked and nothing gained.

Our ninth mission finally happened the following day. We were part of a campaign to bomb the enemy air fields in the area to make the Germans think that we were getting ready for the invasion of the continent. We flew one mission that morning and another that afternoon to bomb Merville and Lille. We were called back on the second attempt for unknown reasons and we never learned what effect the ruse might have had on the German High Command.

REGENSBURG

O N THE SIXTEENTH OF AUGUST, 1943, I went to the orderly room to see if the alert list was made out for the next mission. I arrived just as the operation orders arrived. The orders called for a maximum effort, and the prospective crews were soon posted. For the 349th Squadron there were the names of Barr, Henington, Roane, Van Noy, Justice and the new man, Shotland. He had just moved into the vacant area of our hut. I took the good news back to the hut area as most of the concerned crews were gathered there sweating out the listing. Our crew at that time was made up of the same men we came over to England with; co-pilot Arthur Stipe, bombardier Curtis Campbell, navigator Daniel L. Schmucker and me. With Shotland were co-pilot Charles Thompson, bombardier William Harrison, and navigator Thomas Doran. This would be their first mission.

The pilots of the alerted crews were advised to go to the group briefing room for some poop about our trip the next day. We arrived and were promptly sworn to secrecy regarding what we were about to be told. We were alerted for Regensburg in southern Germany but were not to return to England for a few days. We were advised to take a change of underwear, our class A summer uniform, mess kit, a razor and all other such niceties. The target was a Messerschmitt factory that was producing sixty percent of the ME-109 fighters in which we had no small interest. When we returned to our area, we called a meeting of the crews, including all gunners. The mission information was shared with threats as to how severe the consequences would be for those who talked to anyone. Soon Henington's crew suggested that since we couldn't talk, a crap game might ease the tension. The value of the English pound meant little to us so the stakes didn't seem to be very high.

The new men weren't checked out on the four dollar value of each pound so they were set up for easy picking. My meager stash didn't keep me long in the game so I retired to my bunk to do some reading. Soon afterwards the game ended with some men mumbling to themselves, and I saw Shotland counting his money. He counted three hundred pounds, rolled it up and stuffed it into his footlocker.

Briefing the next morning verified the facts of the first shuttle raid that I had promised our crew. A large portion of additional information was given to us at that time, including the fact that we, the Hundreth Group, would have the unenviable position of low and last (fondly referred to as coffin corner) with a load of 250 pound incendiary bombs. Also, another bit of information that we gained ws that our altitude across the continent was assigned to 17,000 feet. That information we were not at the moment ready to assimilate. It seemed that they mentioned some 300 to 400 enemy fighters would be encountered along the route, but our own P-47s would escort us a far piece along the way.

As if there wasn't enough to mull around in our heads, Sergeant Stuart brought me information to the effect that Ray Tomb, our faithful radio operator, was not present for the trip. I asked Stuart to find us another static chaser, and give him a short briefing if he wasn't already in the know. The proposed change of roster soon brought Captain Veal over to find out what was stirring, as squadron commanders are wont to do. I explained that I didn't know the reason for the failure of my man to show, but I would most certainly be giving him the details if and when. At that strategic time Ray came slinking in and the call for a replacement was canceled. At a later time when we had the occasion to talk, Tomb said he had found a roller skating rink somewhere near and like Cinderella he had lost track of time. He missed the coach home, causing him to walk and run through darkness back to the base. I took that opportunity to caution him about when the wheels are spinning on his feet to not neglect those wheels in his head. I am not sure if I ever related that likely story to Captain Veal or not. Perhaps the events to follow made the excuse unnecessary.

Without much further conversation we went to our trusty old plane "Laden Maiden" where Ray Morton and his crew had just done the preflight inspection and were topping off the gas tanks. He didn't seem to know where we were going as he asked me to be careful with the bird because they didn't want to work all that night patching holes.

A supply truck came by with a bundle of English military style blankets. This gave us a hint as to the accommodations we could expect at the day's end. Morton seemed to want to ask some questions about the action, but he let it be. Another weapons carrier arrived at our hardstand bringing a staff sergeant with a piece of paper in his hand. The paper identified him as a photographer from 8th Air Force Headquarters, and there was a note written on the paper that said the bearer wanted to go along with our crew on the mission. The note was to the attention of "Cowboy" Roane and was signed by "Chick" Harding. I told him to be prepared to spend the night, and to have necessary emergency equipment if he was to be welcomed aboard.

Our usual English weather kept us milling around well past our start engine time. Finally the green flare from the control tower set us moving. In the previous few days we had many hours learning the procedures for climbing as a group through the clouds. The title of our study was Weather SOP. Justice asked me what SOP stood for and I told him I thought it must be Standard Overcast Penetration. Wrong as I was about the title, the study served us well that day. We took off and made our procedural climb, hoping the B-24 group located off the end of our runway 28 would not be doing the same thing at the same time. We broke through the overcast at 4,000 feet and, as wonders would have it, all the group broke through and we rendezvoused. We started our climb but were soon going through another overcast. That climb had a much longer nervous time as we didn't see clearly until we were at 14,000 feet. We broke out still in reasonable formation.

Colonel Curtis LeMay was the Air Boss of the Third Air Division. The division, consisting of seven groups, gathered over Splasher Six, a well know radio locator beacon, and left for Europe at 09:35 Greenwich Mean Time. As we crossed the channel the usual gun and safety checks were made. Our crew was underway on our tenth mission, and it was going to take some drastic malfunction to cause us to break our record of zero aborts. I was, even at that time, a person of the anti-abortion persuasion. One crewman said his gun wasn't working right. I told him not to worry because he probably wouldn't hit anything belonging to the enemy, and he could let the other gunners have his ammo. This individual had recently shot through the tail of a   B-17 in the 100th Bomb Group while on a mission.

Another man said his oxygen regulator wasn't working properly, and I told him to just breathe lightly and at the altitude we were flying he would make it just fine. Campbell called up to say, "Man, those little German kids will be gathering up rocks to hand to the old men to throw at us at the altitude we are flying." Stroble allowed as how the flak would be thick enough that he could get out of the ball turret and walk around on it. Healy made his usual statement, "Boy am I hungry." Actually, as we entered enemy territory, it appeared that the oxygen supply was holding better, the wayward gun no longer was malfunctioning and Healy was soon to get a belly full. The crew had at last settled down for the mission, but that was not to say such serenity would not be fractured by hours of actual fright.

At landfall on the continent we were looking for our P-47 escort, but none were to be seen. Stipe said he saw a group pass overhead possibly going to the head of the division, which gave us some bit of assurance. It was just as well we didn't know that our own "Little Friends" were on the Old Blighty ground still sweating out the weather. It wasn't long though until we realized we were in for a bad time. Stipe announced that Fortresses from the groups up ahead were going down, and we knew it would soon be our turn to enter the fray. Our concentrated combat last for two hours that day. We lived through an estimated 300 fighter attacks. Two squadrons of twelve fighters each climbed to our two o'clock and our ten o'clock positions, turned and flew through our formation with lights rapidly flashing from the leading edge of their wings. We knew that from that time on we would be well engaged. The sound of the guns of the "Laden Maiden" all firing almost continuously was not unlike a Texas tornado passing overhead. When I saw the attacking fighters boring in on us, I couldn't just sit still in my positon so I moved the plane up and down as much as I could within the limits of close formation. Two of the Forts, belonging to Claytor and Hummel, in the last element of the low squadron of our group went down immediately. Also some of the Luftwaffe planes were fallling toward the Fatherland. It has been said that the route of the air battle that day could be traced by burning aircraft on the ground. Any number of parachutes could be seen floating down to earth at almost any time.

As the battle continued, Knox of the lead squadron was observed to leave the formation with two engines out. As they descended, their plane banked and seemed to be heading back the route we had just battled our way along, slowly losing altitude. It was noted that several German fighters were following closely. The fate of that plane and crew are part of the legend of the "Bloody Hundredth."

Healy requested more ammo in the tail as his supply was dwindling. Since the two waist gunners and the camera man were otherwise busy, Tomb said he would take him a couple of belts. Two belts proved to be quite a load at that altitude; however, the delivery was successfully made, and Tomb learned the special value of using a walk around oxygen bottle. While the delivery to the tail was going on, Campbell said he was also running low on ammo. The photographer laid down his movie camera and delivered him an ammunition belt to the nose.

Soon afterwards, Healy reported hitting an FW-190 and seeing it explode. The pilot was seen falling with his parachute burning. It soon failed, letting its occupant go flailing toward the earth. Next, Curtis Biddick's plane, "Escape Kit," just out of my left window and slightly below, had taken a vital hit in the fuselage just behind the co-pilot. Flames engulfed the entire pilot and nose compartments. Two men bailed out of the front escape hatch, but I watched as the co-pilot, Flight Officer Snyder, climbed out on the right wing where he was standing in flames. He reached back into the plane, retrieved his chest pack, put it on and slid off the burning wing. His chute opened too soon and it was caught by the horizontal stabilizer and became entangled. The pilot was still in the airplane as it slipped off to the left, circling while going down with Snyder still dangling in the trapped chute. All of this tragedy soon ended with a large explosion, probably enhanced by the load of incendiary bombs and escaping oxygen.

Healy reported the loss of another B-17 form the second element of the high squadron. Our roommates, Shotland and crew, were going down on their first mission. This wouldn't be the last time we would lose our close friends, and it served as a warning that we all faced death on each and every mission we flew. Braley and crew, flying on Claytor's right wing in "Tweedle O' Twill," came under fighter atack for more than one hour before they had to abandon ship. With number one engine and tail compartment blazing, nine of the men bailed out near Wurzburg, about 125 miles from Regensburg.

At about Mannheim, Germany the battle seemed to have slowed somewhat,and the remaining members of our bomb group moved up into the spots that were left vacant by our recent losses. It was difficult to tell just which planes were still with us. I asked Bud Stipe to take a turn at the wheel and I noted Henington was still there on Barr's right wing. Justice had moved into the lead squadron to fill the spot left open by the loss of Knox. Our crew was in fine shape and the "Laden Maiden" had all engines churning smoothly.

We had been under constant attack for more than an hour, and from aircraft sighting reports, it wasn't over by any means. The target was still many miles away so the brief respite was used to replenish ammunition in the tail and run a station check. We could see some of our own airplanes struggling to keep up with the group, and just perhaps they could make it. The time to target was still sixty more long minutes, and at the target is where we usually could expect the fighters to leave us alone and let the flak have at us, but not today.

Healy reported the presence of an ME-110 at six o'clock level just out of range, hanging on behind. Tomb acknowledged the sighting, and after what seemed to continue five minutes or more the plane trailed us then started moving up. When he came within range of our fifty caliber guns, both Tomb and Healy started firing steadily. The attacker seemed to slow down, fall off to the right and go down trailing heavy smoke. Joe Stroble reported from the ball turret that the plane crashed and exploded. No one had seen a parachute from that particular incident.

Hollenbeck, flying "Flak Happy," on Cleven's left wing in the low squadron was hit in the bomb bay causing premature release of the bomb load. He stayed with the formation until the target was passed and we were over Italy. Not being able to maintain altitude nor airspeed, they went their way alone in the direction of Switzerland. Apparently the trip was not to be, as the entire crew bailed out near Milano.

Near the initial point, just short of high noon, the fighter attacks slowed down, although plenty of enemy planes could be seen in the area. We turned on the bomb run at 11:54 hours with 14 B-17s still in our formation. The target was already clouded with smoke from bombs dropped by the groups of our division that were preceding us. One group, however, was turning away from the target as if they were going to make a circle and attempt another run. But we were determined to get rid of our load of fire bombs as soon as we could. After "bombs away" Oakes dropped out of the formation and headed for what might be Switzerland. He had one propeller feathered and smoke pouring from another engine. We could only hope he made it.

Glen Van Noy had been having problems all during the trip with airplane "Oh Nausea." One of their engines was knocked out in the first part of the air battle and just after the target a second engine failed. We had been briefed that morning, which now seemed days ago, that Sicily might be considered as an emergency crash spot as the Allies would have control that day. The direction taken by the crew would indicate that was what Van Noy had in mind. Fighter opposition had stopped and chances to make Sicily looked good, barring more engine trouble.

We were now on a south heading, and the good aircraft "Laden Maiden" was performing very well. In fact Red Stuart, our engineer, said all gauges were showing the desired settings and we had ample fuel to take us to our destination. I even pulled the fuel mixtures back to lean to make it easier for the engines and fuel supply. Barr, and Captain Veal, flying our lead, had one engine feathered but seemed to have everything under control in "Torchy II." Bob Wolff in "Wolf Pack" was flying along in the lead element with a very sizable chunk out of his horizontal stabilizer; however, with nine planes now missing form the 100th formation, we probably looked much worse than we felt at that time. Usually after the target when Stipe was flying home I could take a little nap, but today I felt like a tourist. The only opposition from Italy was a little token flak as we passed over Lake Garda. As we continued southward toward the Mediterranean Sea, we gradually let down to 10,000 feet altitude, and we started looking for Corsica.

One airplane from one of the other groups continued to descend until he made a splash. We assumed his fuel ran out. He was still afloat when we saw him last. His life raft was deployed and we hoped the best for the crew we left floating. We skirted by Corsica with no enemy activity. Next we flew by Sardinia with continued luck. I suggested that Stroble, our ball turret gunner, climb out and join the rest of us. Joe Stoble was 32 and must be treated as an elderly man deserved.

We were commenting on how beautiful the scenery below us was when another airplane headed for the drink. I wished I could have shared some of our surplus gasoline with him. Africa was dead ahead and the city of Bone became visible. Someone directed that those of us that weren't sweating out fuel should land at Berteaux so those with mechanical and fuel problems could land at Telergma where maintenance support was available. Three of us landed at a flat place in the desert with no runway and no service provided.

There was a French Foreign Legion post there with mules and wagons. Someone brought us some sandwiches of some kind of meat and some water. I wondered if they were making maximum use of their mules. We were soon surrounded by a group of young Arab boys. One very bright lad named Mohammed, of course, took over the conversation. He, after finding out who the "pelot" was, told us that the B-26 had already won the war and moved on. Further that the B-17 was no blanking good. He suddenly stopped short as Stuart took out his partial plate and started cleaning it. Stroble asked him if he didn't know that Americans could all take out their teeth, and to emphasize the point, he removed both of his plates and that cleared the area. The kids stopped some hundred yards away and peered back at us. Soon they departed to go home and share that recently gained knowledge with others.

We slept on the breast of "Mother Earth" that night and found a surprising amount of comfort there. The following day we were directed to fly our airplanes over to Telergma where the division was gathering to assess total damage and to lick its wounds. We were advised to start our engines and taxi to takeoff position without doing our run-up because of the sand. We were striking out on faith that there would be no mechanical problems during our short flight. Things went very well. In fact, we discovered that our plane still flew very well despite 212 holes found in our plane's surface. Some testing was done during the flight, and Stuart, Stipe and I declared the "Maiden" fit for further duty.

On landing at Telergma we were met by Captain Veal who was checking to see if we could fly a combat mission on our return flight to England. I told him that we thought we were in good shape. He then asked me how many flying hours I had accumulated in the B-17. I told him that I had some over 700 hours, whereas he nodded and said that I would be a flight commander thenceforth. Now that was quite an honor for a Flight Officer looking toward his twenty-first birthday, not doubting that he would reach that milestone in his life. After Captain Veal left, Campbell asked me if it were advisable to plan such a long trip over enemy territory with all those many holes in our fuselage and wings. I comforted him by saying that I expected the holes would help us slip through the air.

Another problem became evident when an inspection of the guns was made, revealing that Curtis Campbell's nose gun had been rendered useless by a near melt down of the barrel. I remembered that he was expending an unusually great amount of ammunition by continuous bursts whenever a target presented itself throughout the flight. Since Henington's plane wasn't to fly back home on a combat mission, it was easy to trade him a gun barrel. After the exchange was made, we were again set for a sortie on the way home to Thorpe Abbots.

We were given the task of refueling the airplane with hand crank pumps and fifty-five gallon drums of gasoline. A stakebed truck came out and some Italian prisoners in the back rolled out six 500 pound demolition bombs to fall on the ground at our feet. They smiled and rode away. Another vehicle arrived with a man dispensing fuses which were turned over to Campbell for proper installation in the newly acquired bombs. Before we were long into our reservicing task, a jeep drove up and there dismounted Colonel LeMay. He looked over the crew and asked who the aircraft commander was. I introduced myself and I said I was it. He asked why my men weren't cleaned up and shaved. I explained that no one had pointed out an ablution facility to us. He looked at me and asked where I had found a place to shave to which I answered that I hadn't. He allowed a slight smile to cross his stone face but pointed to a ditch away off and said, "There is a place for your ablutions." We found the necessary place.

On the day scheduled to make our flight home, the pilots went to an informal briefing. I learned only six of the crews from the Hundredth would be able to make the return trip. Justice was one of the few so honored. Several of the others would be flying back around Gibraltar to Thorpe Abbotts. When I returned to the aircraft to prepare for take off, I found the crew fitting an oxygen mask on a small female donkey, as if preparing her for the flight. They thought it was such a good idea that I agreed without knowing any of the procurement details. I decided the animal should be allowed to fly in the radio room to England. When Tomb asked why there, I told him that his spare oxygen mask seemed to be the one that fit her. We decided to name her after Mohammed, the small Arab lad we met earlier. Since there was a difference of gender, we settled for "Mo."

On the twenty-fourth of August, after takeoff, one of the few planes of the group returned to Telergma leaving us with only five to make the homebound trip. The bombing raid back was flown over southwestern France to Bordeaux. I can't recall any fighter oppositon and only meagar flak to contend with. From the target home we were out over water. We had been allowed to see both coasts of France and we decided we liked the latter much better. With everything considered, our crew decided that it was probably the easiest trip we were likely to experience.

When we returned to the base at Thorpe Abbotts, we saw that the aircraft parking areas were nearly all empty. In addition to the sixteen we failed to return with, seven had gone on a raid to France to bomb some German airfields. The ground crews didn't know which bunch was coming in. To several of those men this would be their first realization that their aircraft would not be returning.

As we approached for landing, Stuart fired a red flare indicating we needed medical help. Doc MacCarthy arrived with the medical crew and asked me what the problem was. I told him that I might have a frozen ass. At that time Mo was brought out and turned over to the medics. We taxied on back to our revetment to see Morton and crew somewhat relieved to see us and the "Laden Maiden" even in such bedraggled condition. Without assessing the damage, Ray said that there were some new airplanes arriving the next day, and we might be scheduled to get one. If we did, he and his crew wanted to go over to the new plane and maintain it for us. I agreed that should be one of the conditions of the trade.

Mo and friends

Owen D. Roane

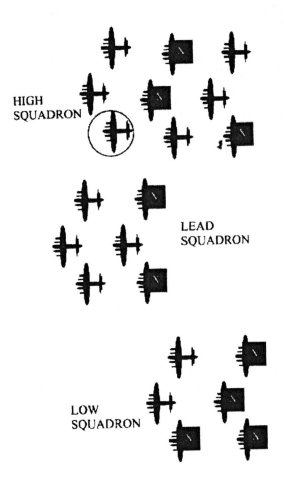

Lead Squadron

No.	Plane Name	Pilots
1.	423393	Just-A-Snappin'	Blakely/Kidd
2.	423327	Stymie	Brady
3.	4230061	Wolf Pack	Wolff
4.	4230066	Mug Wump	Cruikshank/Egan
5.	425860	Escape Kit	Biddick/Curtis*
6.	4230063	Picklepuss	Knox*

High Squadron

No.	Plane Name	Pilots
1.	4230170	Torchy II	Barr/Veal
2.	425861	Laden Maiden	Roane
3.	4230611	Horny	Henington
4.	4230042	Oh Nausea	Van Noy*
5.	423229	Pasadena Nena	Justice
6.	4230002	The WAAC Hunter	Shotland*
7.	425864	Picadilly Lily	Murphy/Lay
8.	4230080	High Life	Oakes*
9.	4230086	Black Jack	Fienup

Low Squadron

No.	Plane Name	Pilots
1.	4230358	Phartzac	Scott/Cleven
2.	423232	Flack Happy	Hollenbeck*
3.	4230335		DeMarco
4.	425867	Alice from Dallas	Claytor*
5.	4230311		Hummel*
6.	4230070	Tweedle O Twill	Braley*

*Missing in Action (MIA)

KING AND I

AUGUST FINALLY ENDED with a flight to Mulan les Meureaux to bomb an aircraft repair depot. The flight was canceled as we neared the outskirts of Paris. Clouds again covered the target area and since it was friendly territory, there would be no random dropping of bombs. We returned home with our cargo. The same load was carried back to France on September the second with the same results. The target this time was to have been the airfield called Kerlin-Bastard. We wondered how it got its name. Finally, the bomb load we had been hauling around was released on the third of September. I was leading the second element of the high squadron so we had a good view of the rest of the group.

Various stories developed concerning what actually occurred on that mission. Our primary target was the Renault Works in Paris, but again the weather was not cooperative. We headed for our secondary target, Beaumont Le Roger Airfield about sixty miles west. Before the bomb run, we were attacked by fighters while being hammered by flak. The second element of the lead squadron consisted of Victor Fienup as leader with Richard King and Charles Floyd as his wingmen. I saw King's ship hit by flak and start burning furiously amidship and fire was enveloping his right wing. As King had been my pilot back in training, I knew the crew well and prayed they would escape. As the plane continured to burn however, it veered into the tail of Floyd, the left wingman, causing him to pull up into the plane flown by Fienup. A large explosion occurred and I saw the airplanes of King and Floyd break up immediately. Fienup's plane went down just moments later.

Peter Theodore, our gunnery officer, went with Floyd's crew, although he was not required to fly on combat missions. As gunnery officer, he thought he should experience the subject he was teaching. Theodore was killed along with the rest of Floyd's crew except the navigator and bombardier, as we later learned.

In addition to that entire element being knocked out, Winleman and Henington from the high squadron were going down. Winkleman was on his first mission and Henington was the first of us four replacements to go down. Henington was flying his plane that was recently christened "Horny," depicting a charging Texas Longhorn steer. Henington had aborted on his first five scheduled missions due to mechanical failure. While discussing a name for his plane, some of us thought "Old Yeller" would be more appropriate.

With those two down, our crew would be alone in the hut. Captain Veal sent us to London on a two day pass while the goods of the two crews were being taken away. Justice had made the trip on my left wing and like the rest of our squadron returned with moderate damage. He said it was number six for him, but he would gain on me while we were in London.

We arrived in London late that evening in time for what remained of a night's sleep. The next morning, we went out to see the sights but weren't prepared for what we saw. Upon going down the subway escalator, we saw some Yank's in well used flying clothes on their way up the companion escalator. It was Henington and crew! Without difficulty, we crossed over the upward moving carriage and soon started our reunion. We learned that on the day before when they were knocked down by debris from our own group's exploding aircraft, they couldn't bail out because Dalton, the navigator, had his chute destroyed. They made it midway into the English channel, ditched their plane, scrambled into their life rafts, and were picked up by a rather small Air Sea Rescue plane of the Royal Air Force. The aircraft "Horny" had vanished into the channel, taking its name and abortive reputation with it.

After picking up Henington's crew, the rescue plane attempted takeoff but fell back into the drink. This process was repeated two more times with the same outcome. Henry told the pilot to take them back to their dinghies and lighten the load. The pilot was afraid to leave them out there in the English Channel so he taxied them all the way back to England. They were on their way back to Thorpe Abbots to retrieve their stuff, and we decided to go back with them. That proved to be a fate tempting move because we arrived in time to be put on alert for Stuttgart.

September the sixth found our group heading out to do damage to an instrument and ball bearing plant at Stuttgart, Germany. The flight down was across France. The weather system covered the ground as we neared the target area. Suddenly, the luck that had been following us seemingly disappeared amid intensive fighter opposition. We were hit in number two engine and a raging fire was started. We pulled the fire extinguisher and cut the fuel to the engine. The prop was feathered, but the fire continued to burn, covering all the wing from number one engine to the cockpit. We were in tight formation and still vivid in my mind was the disaster of our last mission when King exploded taking the others down with him. Were we to suffer the same fate as the crew I had shared so many trying hours with just a few months before? This could happen again with our burning plane to blame.

I told the crew to hang on as we were leaving the formation, and since there were several enemy fighters around to pick off stragglers, I would appear to be falling out of control. I let the plane go into a slow spin, knowing it would soon pick up speed and perhaps the slip stream would blow out the fire of the blazing wing. The gunners couldn't have manned their guns at this point as they were simply holding on for dear life. Campbell called to announce our air speed had passed three hundred miles per hour and Stuart happily told us the fire was out. Relaxing my grasp on the wheel, the good old "Laden Maiden" righted itself just as we were dropping into the cloud deck. Since we were still over

Germany, Campbell released our bomb load to let the chips fall where they may. Stipe and I enjoyed flying instruments for a change. Things were looking good so I asked Schmucker to give us a vector for home. He gave us a northwesterly heading and we were breathing normally again.

Healy announced that he was hungry.

Suddenly, what we usually wished for happened. The overcast ended leaving us sitting high and dry. There we were, cruising along on three engines in broad daylight at around ten thousand feet, feeling rather foolish. I announced I would get us out of that situation by losing our surplus altitude. We leveled off at about fifty feet above the terrain and continued on our heading. A large city was ahead so we went far to the right of it. Schmucker said the city was Antwerp. Campbell allowed that several chickens in the area would not be laying for weeks. Healy was looking for military targets to expend his fifty caliber ammunition on, but I told him to not stir up the ground defense people too much as we had to depart the area over water soon and there would be no hiding place there.

We evidently left the continent near the border of Holland and Belgium. I decided to skid the aircraft to prevent a potentially good marksman of the coastal artillery batteries form lining up on us. At that low altitude, I couldn't bank the plane because the wings were clipping the waves. Fortunately, we had no action against us, so within a few miles we were able to start our climb, turn on our IFF, and cruise home at about three thousand feet. We saw the balloon hangar at Pulham and joined some of our planes in landing at Thorpe Abbotts. At debriefing, we found that no one reported our departure from the group as there was plenty of other information to occupy their accounts.

We learned that after we departed the group, it was divided, and ten went back to bomb Conches Air Field in France. At that point, the Luftwaffe atttacked again and knocked five of the Fortresses out of formation. The first of the planes lost at Conches was flown by Walter Grenier on his first mission. Sam Turner and Edgar

Woodward went toward Switzerland. Sumner Reeder and Arthur
Vetter were limping back toward England. In all, six planes were
lost from the Hundredth due to enemy action with three, including
our own, making it back to England sporting extensive damage.
Vetter and I were able to return to Thorpe Abbotts as we had
manageable aircraft damage, but Reeder landed at the first base in
England, with the co-pilot, Harry Edeburn, dead and three other of
his crew gravely injured.

Looking back over the last two missions, King and I were not
destined to share the same fate; however, a few hours earlier my
crew did not dare believe otherwise. Of King's crew that was lost
on the previous mission, we had the report that only Engineer
Trafford Curry survived. This information was brought back to
Thorpe Abbotts by Curry himself who had bailed out early and
was able to evade. I was sad about the fate of the rest of the crew
as I had become exceptionally close to the whole bunch before I
went with my own men. At our reunion in Dayton, Ohio in 1985, I
saw a man that I thought was dead. Edward Hovde, the
bombardier of King's plane was standing in the lobby of the hotel.
I asked him what happened as I had seen their plane explode. He
said he wasn't sure, but he regained consciousness while lying on
part of an airplane wing. He was able to pull his ripcord in time to
cushion his fall. He said he must have had his left hand on his left
knee when the explosion occurred because they were both severed
and he was bleeding profusely. He was immediately picked up by
German troops and taken to the hospital where he spent about three
months in recovery before being repatriated to the United States.
He told me the navigator, Anderson, bailed out successfully and
was taken prisoner. "Andy" came to the reunion at Long Beach
and the three of us spent some time reliving the incident. I also
learned that Heber Hogge and Jim Sides made it out of the plane
and were taken prisoners. They were released after the Germans
surrendered. They told me that Barney Sutton was not on the
flight as he had returned to the States for pilot training. I was

aware of this because Barney came by to visit me at my home in Valley View, Texas, but our renewed friendship sadly was not to be lasting. He died a few short months later.

We were called into the briefing room on September the seventh to make a run over to France and bomb the airfield at Watten again. It was an easy run that took only four hours.

We celebrated Italy's surrender on the ninth of September by flying again over France on some kind of scare tactics. We hit the Beauvais airport that morning with much success. That afternoon, we went again to an airfield near Arth, but could not drop our bombs because of overcast conditions. We did not get credit for a mission that afternoon as the powers that were decided we were not deserving a relative freebie.

When we got back to the base, Doctor McCarthy told us he had gotten a three day pass for our crew. He looked at me and said, "you won't be going though, because of your color. You will probably get a long rest in the regional hospital." I had somehow managed to contract hepatitis, or as we at home called it, yellow aundice. I knew cleaning up in that branch water in Africa would do me no good. I told the crew good-bye and God go with them, but I was not really yellow. Stuart told me, "I know, and I'm not flying with anyone but you, Cowboy."

Anderson   Hovde   King

King's Crew at Wendover

Owen D. Roane

BREMEN

O N OCTOBER THE THIRD I finally returned to Thorpe Abbotts. I had just spent time from September the ninth to October the third in the regional hospital recovering from jaundice. Doctor McCarthy (Mack the Quack) prescribed one month bed rest, but I made such a nuisance of myself at the hospital that they discharged me early. Before I arrived home on the fourth, most of my crew left with Lieutenant Brooks on a jmission to Hanau, Germany. As Jack Herlihy thought that I should return to the saddle right away, he let me fly "slow time" with a plane that had just had an engine change. I took the crew chief along as co-pilot and as many of the men nearby, of the ground persuasion, who desired and could find a parachute. While I was thus flexing my wings, the Group returned without "Pinky" Helstom, one of the original pilots. I "slow timed" again on the sixth with most of my own crew.

On the seventh we were alerted for a trip to Bremen, Germany, which seemed like a reasonably safe mission. But due to heavy rainstorms in East Anglia that morning, the mission was postponed. Later, when the weather cleared, we were allowed to participate in such training as necessary. When that occasion was finished, we returned to the base to learn that Bremen was on again. The Hundredth Group was to lead the 13th Combat Wing. The 95th and the 390th were assigned to complete the wing formation. Major Jack Kidd and Captain Everett Blakely with the 418th Squadron were flying lead. Captain Alvin Barker with Captain Thomas Murphy were to fly in the low squadron with the 351st. Major Gale Cleven and Captain Bernard DeMarco were assigned the high squadron, and Flight Officer Owen "Cowboy" Roane with Lieutenant Arthur Stipe were taking the 349th for the third element of the high squadron and spare aircraft.

Our crew for the Bremen Mission was:

Flight Officer Owen D. Roane .... Pilot
Lieutenant Arthur C. Stipe .... Co-pilot
Lieutenant Omar Gonzales .... Navigator
Lieutenant Curtis K. Campbell .. Bombardier
Sergeant Robert A. Stuart .... Engineer
Sergeant Richard Dettweiler .. Asst. Engineer
Sergeant Clarence R. Tomb .. Radio Operator
Sergeant Roger O. Stroble .... Ball Turret
Sergeant James Jarvie .... Waist Gunner
Sergeant Patrick J. Healy .... Tail Gunner

Other 349th crews flying with us that day were: Lieutenant Arthur H. Becktoft flying my left wing, Lieutenant John K. Justice flying my right wing, Lieutenant Henry M. Henington filling a position in the lead squadron, Lieutenant Edward G. Stork filling a position in the lead squadron, and Lieutenant Robert N. Lohof filling a position in the high squadron.

Stuart

Jarvie

Tomb

Stroble

Healey

Hauge

Our assigned aircraft, "Laden Maiden," was not well, and since Sammy Barr was not flying that day, I was given "Torchy III" for the trip to Bremen. With some trepidation, we left the well-maintained Maiden for an unknown. It turned out that we had no need to worry in that respect because Torchy did great. I will forever be grateful for Jack Herily and his "Merry Men" as I have no doubt that much of the credit for our being able to complete our tour was due to them. No single mission flown by our crew was cut short because of mechanical failure. When we took off, we went all the way. That was a major accomplishment as so many aborts were occurring during those months and, the big majority of the time, mechanical failure was given for the reason. The abort rate was becoming an embarrassing, if not dangerous, factor within the 8th Bomber Command.

On the mission to Bremen, the groups' assembly was done smoothly and at 1330 hours they were all under way on a heading o 080 degrees. Bud Stipe commented that all four of the first replacement crews were in the formation. We always tried to keep close watch on the other three: Henington, Justice and Walter Moreno of the 350th Squadron. We had arrived in England generally at the same time as the rest of the 100th Group, but it never occurred to us to ask why we all four were readily accepted. We had no way of knowing that the day before, the Hundredth had lost three planes on their first mission. My friends looked askance at me when we learned the fact. We all now had between ten and twelve sorties, but sadly this would be the last time all four of us flew on combat mission together.

We leveled off at 25,000 feet in very good formation and routine station checks were made. Test firing of the guns was accomplished. Stipe reported we were near the enemy coast and all gunners should be on alert. Healy made his normal comment, "Boy am I hungry." I never asked him the real meaning of his comment. In the distance, it was noted that German Fighters and some P-47 fighters were having it out while two of the advanced wings were under fighter attack. The 13th Wing, however, experienced only three attacks directed against the 390th Group during the first ten minutes over enemy territory.

The range of our escort must have been reached because what looked like at least a hundred enemy fighters were just in time to greet us at the front of our formation. Then Stipe said, 'Bandit at eleven o'clock coming straight at us." Due to our position, our gunners couldn't get any rounds off, but Stroble and Healy were waiting for him to pass under the formation so they could get clear shots. He didn't pass under because he hit the B-17 flying the number six position of the low squadron. A large explosion and falling pieces were all that could be seen except one parachute. There went "Marie Helena." The wingman of the FW-190 that hit Gormley passed over our group and under the 95th, although somewhere between the two groups his plane exploded. I was of the opinion our top turret, manned very effectively by "Red" Stuart, had a large part in the kill.

One moment later, the lead aircraft of the second element of the high squadron, just some 200 feet ahead of our airplane, exploded leaving debris for the rest of the high squadron to fly through. That plane, piloted by Frank Meadows, was probably destroyed by the detonation of its own bombs. Reports say the wings and tail all went in different directions. Just moments later "War Eagle," flown by Arthur Becktoft, flying my left wing, left the formation under control with number three engine blazing violently. In less than four minutes from our first encounter, our group had lost three aircraft, but the worst was yet to come.

At 1521 hours our group reached the Initial Point and turned to a heading of 046 degrees. James Douglass, Bombardier of the lead plane opened his bomb bay doors, and the rest of the group followed suit. We had closed up the formation as best we could with the missing aircraft being compensated for, and the bomb run had begun. From this point until the Rally Point our group encountered the most intense, accurate flak barrage we had eve experienced. The next five minutes to target were the most vulnerable ones of the trip as far as flak was concerned. Flying straight and level through the gauntlet was always a nervous time, but today was extreme. The target, Bremen, could easily be detected by an intense black cloud marking it, courtesy of smoke pots and fire and smoke from bomb strikes of the previous wings.

Moments after the group had lined up on the bomb run, the sky occupied by the 100th erupted from another massive flak barrage. "Picadilly Lily," piloted by Barker and Murphy, received heavy damage to the nose section but continued to the drop point as the lead of the low squadron. Shortly after "Bombs Away," the Lily had more hits and the plane seemed to shake as a fire appeared immediately from the number two engine. Murphy pulled out of formation to start abandoning the ship. Barker was reported to have said, "Let's get the hell out of this crate, she's gonna blow." The chute of the first man failed to open, five open chutes were counted, then the plane disintegrated in an explosion.

Just one moment later, "Salvo Sal" flown by Lieutenant William MacDonald in number four positon of the high squadron, lost one engine and fell behind. He tried to join the 95th Group but was attacked by fighters and lost another engine. The crew abandoned their aircraft and nine chutes were counted. The loss of this fifth plane, three from the high squadron, left the rest of us scurrying for a positon. To add to the mess, Nash, flying in number six spot of the high squadron, was obviously having trouble keeping up, causing myself and Justice to lag. Not wanting to play the "Lonesome Dove," Jack pulled down and moved up to the lead squadron. Now Nash was not going to be able to keep up and I couldn't abide my resultant position. So I made other arrangements. I saw the 95th Group approaching above and from the rear. I pushed the throttles forward and all four engines responded well. Minus the bombs, half the fuel and much ammo, the plane, "Torchy III," made a rapid climb.

As we neared the formation, I realized the rate of closure was much more than was needed. I eased off on the throttles but the excess speed was still a problem. I pulled the throttles all the way back and settled into place but had to rapidly apply power to keep the desired spot. I have often wondered since, why I didn't have a supercharger runaway. Stuart in the top turret was having an extra nervous condition and said it looked like the planes on either side and above us were going to run into us. I don't think I ever fully explained the actual situation. Why cause him to have doubts about his pilot? Stipe quietly observed the maneuver and felt the same relief that I did in our new position. In fact, he seemed happy to take his turn piloting at that time. We were filling the diamond of the lead squadron in our adopted group. After crossing the Channel, we bid a fond farewell and rejoined the remainder of the 100th for landing. I thanked Torchy's ground crew for such a well maintained aircraft, and I explained the stress I had put the bird through.

Debriefing was a sad occasion. Eight of our aircraft had not returned. Many Monday morning article writers would declare that morale was at its lowest, but that had nothing to do with the morale. It is to my mind normal to mourn the loss of your comrades-in arms. It did not in any way mean that we were less determined to carry the air war forward. From the 349th we had lost Arthur Becktoft's crew and, as squadron leader, I was especially concerned. Further, the officers of his crew shared the space in our crew's quonset hut. This would make the third time that supply people would come by and pick up the belongings of our hut mates. Some good news came as we were preparing to return to the squadron area. Kidd, Blakely and crew had crashed at another base in England and all were safe. We reluctantly trudged back to the quarters we had left some seventeen hours earlier and, as we arrived at the opening in the woods that marked home, we saw the truck backed up to our door. "The supply man cometh."

According to Jim Brown's records, eight planes did not return, and nine of those that did return had varying degrees of damage. "Hot Spit," piloted by Edward Stork, returned with two of her engines feathered, one that wouldn't feather, and the good engine was discovered to have been hit by flak. "Messie Bessie," piloted by Chief Walter Moreno, had her rudder smashed. "Sunny II," piloted by John Griffin, experienced an exploding 20mm shell that blew off the top of the upper turret, hurling the engineer into the gangway leading to the nose compartment. After landing, the crew found bullet holes in all four props.

In all, the group had lost seventy-two combat crewmen and at least thirteen were hospitalized suffering from wounds. The gunners of the group claimed sixteen enemy fighters. There was a time during the flight that I had wondered about the possibility that my return from the hospital had been premature.

Formation Chart
Bremen

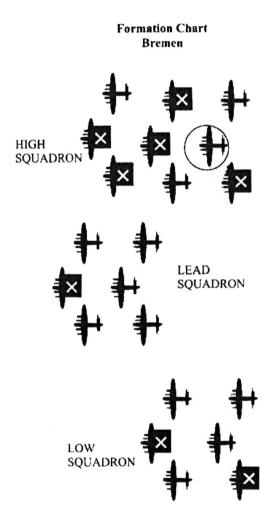

MUNSTER

AFTER THE MISSION TO BREMEN our crew was offered a three day pass and we took it. Although I had flown only the Bremen mission since returning from the hospital, most members of my crew had been flying steadily with Lieutenant Brooks and by now had accumulated twenty-two missions, with the exception of Stuart and Tomb, who had nineteen. Campbell and Stipe wanted to go ahead and finish up, but decided not to tempt fate. They went with the rest of us on pass. Justice told me he was going to catch up with me as he had fifteen missions and I had only eighteen. We were pushing each other to see who would be second to finish. Glenn Dye had just finished his twenty-five missions and was returning home.

We left the base just before a maximum effort mission alert was called. We normally went to the Red Cross Club near Oxford Circle in London, but this time we had heard of a place where some ancient men called Druids were supposed to have erected some very large stones for some ancient reason. We went to visit that place before the weather got too bad for outdoor excursions; therefore, we missed an attempt to recall us to the base. We journeyed to look at the large stones, but after seeing them for ten inspiring minutes, and finding nothing else in the area of interest for young American tourists, we returned to London. After viewing the devastation caused by the latest German air raids, we decided to go back home.

We arrived at Thorpe Abbotts on the tenth of October to learn that our group had made a raid the previous day on Marienburg with only thirteen available airplanes. They all returned and the results were excellent. The target was a very large aircraft plant that produced FW-190 fighters, so the report was good news.

Justice had made the trip and was at that very time on a mission to Munster, Germany to try to disrupt the railhead to the Ruhr Valley. It seems that most of the railroad workers were housed there. That would make seventeen missions for him. This very important Munster effort must be included in my writings, even though I was not a participant.

Our crew bicycled out to meet and congratulate Justice's crew on return, or as we called it, "sweating them out." After a while the weather started moving in and it was going to be difficult to land. One plane from the 390th came in with a Hundredth plane with two engines out following him. It was one of the new crews with a pilot named Rosenthal. The men were whisked off to debriefing. A few more planes from other groups landed at Thorpe Abbotts. We gave up on the rest of our group and supposed they had landed at another base due to the English weather.

Another collection of men was at the parking area awaiting the return of the 100th. It was Robert Hughes and his crew. They had been scheduled to make the trip to Munster but had to come back from the run-up area, as there was a prohibited drop in the magneto of one engine. It was caused by a broken sparkplug wire, a casualty of the last mission. They were rushed to a new plane, which was purported to be combat ready, but it was discovered that the guns were still preserved in cosmoline. A rush cleaning ensued and they made a delayed takeoff in time to catch up with the formation. When the guns were checked over the English Channel, it was found that only seven of the thirteen guns would operate. Additional attempts at cleaning were made until well within France, to no avail. At this time Major Egan, the group command pilot, advised Hughes to return to Thorpe Abbotts and they would see them when they got back. Hughes was of the second bunch of replacement crews. He arrived on the fourth of July while I was on my first mission. By now we were getting to be "Old Timers."

Later that evening we learned that the other crews would not be coming back. Years later I got the story from my friend, Jack Justice, so it seems fitting for him to finish this mission report. His story is:

"The 100th Bomb Group which became operational in May, 1943, had participated in missions on the 8th and 9th of October and had sustained losses in aircraft and personnel to such an extent that on the Munster raid (the 10th of October) they were able to put only twelve planes in the air instead of a complete group of eighteen to twenty-one. The other six or nine aircraft were to be supplied by another Bomb Group, but they never appeared, or else they returned to their base.

The practice of the Germans was to concentrate on the weakest unit and on the 10th of October 1943, the 100th appeared the weakest with only twelve planes in formation.

We were over Germany and had been under attack for some time when our group leader was hit and his airplane caught fire. The pilot performed the prescribed procedure of putting his nose down and getting away from the formation. His wing man, according to procedure, should have taken over the formation lead; instead, all five ships in his squadron followed him down, leaving our low squadron with three aircraft. The Germans immediately came in at all of us and split the remaining formation all over the sky. We found ourselves completely alone. I observed a group to our left returning from the target area. They were some five or six miles away and lower so we dove to meet them and joined their formation, taking a position between all three squadrons. It was a presumably safe place and we headed homeward. Shortly thereafter a Jerry attacked this group and was aiming, I am sure, at the lead aircraft. Instead, he hit our number four engine with a 20mm shell which knocked it completely out and sent us in a flat spin.

From approximately 20,000 feet, John, the co-pilot, and I tried to pull the aircraft out and, at about 5,000 feet we succeeded, but we were still in a dive. John and I continued to try to right the aircraft and leveled off below 1,000 feet, at which time it was apparent that the rest of the crew members had parachuted out. We counted seven chutes, and John tried to stop the engineer from going out the bomb bay, but the engineer could not hear him and abandoned the aircraft.

John and I, without discussing it, decided to head for home, crewless and crippled. The number four engine was still on the aircraft, but there was no cowling all the way back into the wing. We were able to control the aircraft and John decided to take up position in the upper turret, to protect us from any further attack. We had no communication so it was my supposition that John, upon entering the turret, saw a German following us down and turned the turret to take aim. The German seeing the turret move, realized that there was still life aboard and sprayed us from one wing tip to the other with 20mm shells. Both wings were completely on fire and the whole side of the cockpit, my side, was blown away.

John, realizing our situation, came forward from the upper turret. There was blood across his forehead. He reached under my seat, handed me my barrel chute, then put his on and went out through the bombardier's hatch. I put on my chute and went toward the bomb bay. The turret had been turned so I was unable to get out that way. I turned around and, for some reason, I stepped back up into the cockpit to retrieve something and then proceeded down and out the bombardier hatch. To this day I do not know what it was I took form the cockpit. I was not over 500 feet in the air when my chute opened. All I could see below me were trees and one sandy patch ahead. I decided to try to land in the sand. Having had instructions on how to guide a chute, I grabbed an armful of shroud lines hoping to make the sandy area, but found I was going away from it. I let go of the shroud lines and decided to let well enough alone and go into the trees.

Fortunately for me, the trees in this area were planted and were all the same size and just about two feet higher than my collapsed chute. I did not hit the ground, but rather hung in the trees, with my feet just about two feet in the air. I received no scratches, bruises or injuries of any sort, with the exception of a wound on the back of my neck, which had occurred when the side of the cockpit had been blown away. I unbuckled my chute harness and dropped to the ground. About that time approximately one mile to the south of me the aircraft crashed.

I always knew that to abort on a mission without really good reasons was equivalent to turning and running when your army squad on the ground was under intense enemy attack. Especially when the Luftwaffe was always alert to any groups with less than a full complement of planes. Where were all the other crews that had pilots with names very familiar to the group? At least ten experienced crews that weren't on flak leave didn't make the trip. I am proud to say when our crew was scheduled for a mission, we went without any individual aborts."

Justice's escape from the Occupied Europe is another story. He was the first, and as fate would have it, the only one of us four early replacements to be reported as missing in action.

It would be hard not having him around to aggravate. I remembered that I had recommended the 100th Bomb Group to him as a good unit for duty, and I am sure he hated me for my urging. Little did I know that we would be flying together again in just five years taking food and supplies to these very same German people. We just by fate came to Europe again on the same special orders to fly the "Berlin Airlift." As an afterthought I am sure the residents of Berlin were happy that we survived duty in World War II despite their effort otherwise.

Jack Justice and escape route

SCHWEINFURT

FOUR DAYS AFTER the Munster catastrophe, our crew was called to briefing for another mission. Our briefing room was not crowded, because there seemed to be almost as many on stage to tell us how to fly the mission as there were participants in the venture. Scheduled as Air Boss of the Hundredth Bomb Group was not a colonel, major, captain nor lieutenant. It befell a lowly Flight Officer called Cowboy Roane. It was great to have such trust placed on such a young, insignificant member of the group. It would be another quick thrust into Pas de Calais in all probability. It seemed strange that only a hand full of crews was in the audience, and none of the old time warriors of the originals were there with their overwhelming presence. I knew we were short of aircraft and crews since the drastic reductions we had experienced earlier in October, but the showing here seemed to emphasize the negative.

Eight crews stood at attention when Colonel Harding took the stage. We were advised that our effort today would do much to shorten the war. Too bad the dependable leaders were going to miss out on the honor of this day. He wished us good luck and good bombing and took his seat rather abruptly. Major Minor Shaw next took the stand with his long, but not too long, pointer to show us the way. On opening the curtain we were all surprised when our red string route designation did not lead to the French coast but stretched far beyond. It stretched past Brussels, Belgium to a point deep into Germany. When our eyes became fairly focused on the turnaround, we saw an old familiar town named Schweinfurt. Time for reminiscing would come later on at "THE BIGASSBIRD II," as we must now lend an ear to the briefing.

Beyond Aachen, Germany, the First Air Division with some hundred and sixty planes was to fly along a course just north of a direct track while the Third Air Division with like number of bombers would turn south, flying along the Belgian-German border. The First Division was to draw off most enemy fighters as it flew to a point north of Frankfort am Main, where it would take a southeasterly course to its Initial Point (IP) just southwest of Schweinfurt. The Third Division was to continue to fly south along the Belgian-German border to Luxembourg then turn back toward the target arriving just after the First Division had dropped their bombs. The Second Division with sixty B-24s was to take a more southerly direction and arrive in Schweinfurt immediately after we of the Third Division had departed the target.

The route we were to take would detour around the heavy concentrations of flak and we were to have P-47 escort to almost the point we would turn south, in case enemy fighters chose our Division for devastation. We were briefed for 350 single engine enemy fighters with a generous sprinkling of twin engine fighters lobbing missiles at us. I was to take our group to rendezvous with the Thirteenth Combat Wing, with four of us joining the 390th Bomb Group and Lieutenant Robert Hughes would lead the other four planes to join the 95th Bombardment Group. We were assured the other groups would be expecting us and they had reserved spaces for us to join the party. We hoped they wouldn't put us too far away from the orchestra. Weather would be as weather was expected to be over England. We would climb through the clouds and be in the clear when time came to join our sponsoring groups.

Briefing was soon over with time for those individuals wishing to have another or first time meeting with their respective chaplains. Happily, there were enough Sky Pilots to administer almost individually to those needing help. Most members of my crew had already made their peace with God soon after learning our destination that day. It didn't strain our memory to recall what had happened at Schweinfurt just two months before.

We had an abundance of transportation to take us out to our plane with no one having to hang on the side or ride on the hood. I got to know our navigator for the trip much better during our walk around to kick the tires. He was Omar Gonzales who had been recently aced out of his position as Group Navigator. He replaced Daniel Schmucker who had taken this opportunity to go to Wing and start teaching how to fly and bomb with the benefit of RADAR, whatever that was. But the benefit of his services would be for the last time, sadly, because on the fifth of November, Omar and the other non pilot members of the crew he was flying with were given the opportunity of walking back to Thorpe Abbotts from somewhere deep within the Rhur Valley. The aircraft they were on was deemed to be unfit for further flight; however, the two pilots, Gossage and Flesh, found the lighter plane could struggle on, so they returned to our base in England. When I left Thorpe Abbotts to return to the States, Omar had not yet made it back.

One other man went with us that day and for the rest of my missions. He was the assistant engineer who replaced one of my waist gunners that was having trouble distinguishing Spitfires from enemy fighters. He finally was assured of a new career in the Air Corps when he assaulted my wingman with a fifty caliber machine gun. He was reassigned to the Military Police detachment. The new man was Richard O. Dettweiler, and he became flight engineer after Robert Stuart finished his missions. Dettweiler had previously flown with another pilot of the Group who had his wings shot off on a mission, so he couldn't fly anymore. I am positive that I never wore mine in combat missions.

Before loading onto the aircraft I passed some time with Campbell. He was the same cheerful and assuring member of the team. He said, "Roane, we are not going to get back from this mission." I thanked him for his reassurance. Jim Brown tells the Schweinfurt story thus:

"On the 14th, a Thursday, the decision was taken to attack the ball bearing plants at Schweinfurt. As usual the details were transmitted by teletype and were followed by a cryptic message from General Anderson, of Eighth Bomber Command: 'This air operation today is the most important air operation yet conducted in the war. The target must be destroyed. It is of vital importance to the enemy...'

"As for the Hundredth, the Thirteenth Combat Wing released its bombs through flak and smoke at 1454 with 'excellent results,' with the 390th 'being the most successful group.' Despite the rockets and constant fighter attacks, the planes made it back to the French coast, crossing at 1645, to make for Beachy Head, from where despite clouds and poor visibility, the crews located Thorpe Abbots.

"For once the Century Bombers had been lucky. They were the only Group not to have suffered injury or loss, although the gunners put in a claim for seven enemy fighters. The crews were amazed as the story slowly unfolded – sixty B-17's were missing and five had crashed on their return. Twelve more were written off in crash landings, or were only fit for scrap, while 121 required repairs.

"In all, nearly 600 men were missing, while five dead and nearly fifty wounded were taken out of the planes on their return. As for the damage, three of the bearing plants were heavily hit and it took six months before two returned to full production. Work at the largest, the Kugelfischer Plant, was only stopped for six weeks."

While the foregoing report is interesting and correct, perhaps a bird's eye view of the matter would help do justice for this very significant mission . . .

Our crew chief and all the other ground personnel seemed to be extra solicitous of our crew that day. Did they suspect or otherwise have a clue to the magnitude of our pending venture? At any rate our engine start and taxi out seemed to be a more solemn occasion than usual. Despite the weather, we were green lighted and made our takeoff. I collected our meager formation and headed for rendezvous with the 390th, which were just where they were supposed to be, though at a different alititude because of the weather over East Anglia. Anglia being the place where angels dwell, perhaps we could have invisible additions to our formation because the Thirteenth Combat Wing now consisted of two visible groups instead of three.

Before we departed the Island, our Wing leader tucked us into the lead Wing as though we were part of it. He slowed down on right turns and increased speed on left turns to remain in tight formation all the way to the IP. The lower Wing had only two groups and took similar actions so the Third Division appeared as one larger than normal combat wing. Whether or not this maneuver worked to our benefit, I recall losing only one B-17 from our Division enroute to the target. We did see one fighter group of P-47's lending penetration support, but no P-38's or Spitfires.

The leaders of our effort were unknown to me at the time; however, they became known to me as I wrote this account. Leading the Third Division was Colonel Archie Olds, whom I knew later in the Strategic Air Command as General Archie Olds, and leader of our composite 390th Wing was Colonel Thomas Jeffery, who later became Commander of the Hundredth Bomb Group.

Apparently the First Division bore the brunt of the Luftwaffe anger during the trip in to target because the many attacks we endured during that phase of the mission seemed to be of single fighter sweeps. Also those passes were going overhead or breaking off before getting into close range of our gunners. Usually they would come at us in echelon and quite often fly through our formation with their guns blinking. No doubt our close division formation discouraged that approach.

We reached the IP despite the flak. We dropped our bombs with the 390th leader, so all praises for plastering the target was theirs. Campbell said it appeared to be in the barrel, so let's get out of here. The road back was rife with difficulties. The Luftwaffe, having tired of making destruction with the First Division, were now giving us their attention. I saw one plane of our adopted group going down but otherwise we were hanging in close and returning fire toward all those venturing into range. No need to consider aircraft identification of those little spiteful creatures because they all meant us harm. The prevailing westerly winds were also our enemy this day but I knew of nothing that any of us could do about that.

The German fighters had time to refuel at various service stations along our track and were now coming at us in mournful numbers, as Curtis Campbell would quote to us. Still we of the Thirteenth Combat Wing prevailed. One other plane went down from the 95th formation which Tom Hughes' troop had joined, but fate again smiled on members of the Hundredth. We all made it home. I said, "Another day; another dollar." Another remark was heard, "Boy am I hungry." We learned later the number of enemy aircraft that we encountered that "Black Thursday" was in the neighborhood of one thousand. That was a bad neighborhood to be found in.

After we made it to the area where we could see that lovely Island called England on return from the Schweinfurt mission, Campbell talked to the other short timers, Healy, Jarvie, Stoble and Stipe and allowed that there wasn't any way they could make two more missions. Stipe said not to talk about it. Our ground personnel showed relief and happiness that we had returned to our parking area. I am sure they were not looking forward to working the bugs out of another new airplane, nor having to put up with another crew.

Months later I received orders assigning myself and the rest of our four crews, namely Captain Robert Lohoff and crew, Captain William Lankin and crew and Captain Don Mitchell and crew to the 390th Bombardment Group for the Schweinfurt mission. This made us all eligible for the Presidential Distinguished Unit Citation, as the 390th were so cited for action that day. As for those who never saw the order and citation, I will include a copy of each in this delayed journal for a permanent record for them.

Veal   Roane   Healy

Distinguished Flying Cross

Owen D. Roane

HEADQUARTERS ARMY AF

STATION NO. 139, AP0559

CORRECTED COPY   27 March 1945
Special Orders
Number 82

EXTRACT

1.   VOCO, this Hq, 14 Oct 43, ordering, "The fol O & EM, orgns indicated, WP
      mil acft w/o delay fr AAF Sta 139 to AAF Sta 153, on tdy for one
      (1) day with 390 Bomb Gp. For purpose of operational mission.
      CTRS.

100th Bomb Group (H)

CAPT OWEN D ROANE,   02044848
1ST LT ARTHUR C. STIPE,   0677303
1ST LT OMAR GONZALES,   0725967
1ST LT CURTIS CAMPBELL,   0739070
T Sgt Robert A Stuart,   35480233
T Sgt Richard Dettweiler,   17076709
T Sgt Roger O Stoble,   35404098
T Sgt Clarence R Tomb,   13098719
T Sgt Patrick J Healy,   33328163
T Sgt James Jarvie,   13112633
CAPT ROBERT H LOHOF,   0533023
CAPT WILLIAM VADEN,   0736818
1ST LT ROBERT PHILLIPS,   0743495
1ST LT PAUL T DAVIS,   0670034
T Sgt Sidney Goldenburg,   12135177
T Sgt Guy L Brown, Jr.,   36516549
S Sgt Richard L David,   15320263
S Sgt Vern R Lines,   39531989
S Sgt James M Butler,   12146229
S Sgt George W Briggs,   39193615

CAPT WILLIAM G LAKIN,   0740839
1ST LT YANDELL S WARREN,   0802500
1ST LT CARL M DAVIDSON,   0523333
1ST LT ROBERT G MILAM,   0683284

T Sgt John K Beard,   13063333
T Sgt Charlea A Maybe,   31184405
S Sgt Fay A Hulsey,   38161566
S Sgt Clarence A Butts,   16062813
S Sgt Eugene A Beister,   37259779
S Sgt Daniel F Feagins,   38270290

CAPT DON M MITCHELL,   0672383
1ST LT EARL G HAFIN,   0676264
1ST LT KEITH A SPRAGUE,   0746210
1ST LT DUNCAN McCORMIC,   0673802
Pvt John J Boggs,   34035914
S Sgt Harold F Hodgdon,   31163212
S Sgt Donald A McAllister,   6557179
T Sgt James W Cunningham,   13039826
S Sgt Alfred J Michini,   13044380
S Sgt Thomas A Kendall,   12200107

(Auth: VOCO, Hq 3rd Air Division, 113, Oct 43.),'' is hereby confirmed and made a matter of record. The exigencies of the service precluded the issuance of written orders in advance.

*   *   *   *   *   *

BY ORDER OF
COLONEL SUTTERLIN

HORACE L. VARIAN, JR.
Major, Air Corps,
Adjutant

GENERAL ORDERS)   WAR DEPARTMENT
            NO. 30)   WASHINGTON, D.C.
                                        8 April, 1944.

Owen D. Roane

EXTRACT

XI--BATTLE HONORS.--As authorized by Executive Order No. 9306 (sec. I, Bull. 22, WD, 1943) Superseding Executive Order No. 9075 (sec. III, Bull. 11, WD, 1943), citation of the following units by the Commanding General, Eighth Air Force, under the provisions of section IV, Circular No. 333, War Department, 1943, in the name of the President of the United States as public evidence of deserved honor and distinction, are confirmed. The citation read as follows:

*   *   *   *   *   *

The 390th Bombardment Group (H), United States Army Air Forces in the European theater of operations, is cited for conspicuous battle action and extraordinary heroism in connection with the highly successful bombing mission over Schweinfurt, Germany, 14 October 1943. Sixty aircraft of the United States Army Air Forces were lost that day. At the time of the mission, the ball and roller bearing plant at Schweinfurt was designated as the most important target in Germany. The three plants comprising the objective accounted for over 50 percent of Germany's entire supply of ball and roller bearings, which are essential to all makes of aircraft, tanks, and other mobile military equipment. The operation involved a flight of 7 hours and 10 minutes duration, and covered a total flying distance of 925 miles. Over 370 of these miles were flown without friendly fighter support. Carefully planned and savagely executed German fighter attacks persisted from the time the group reached Luxembourg until it was over the Channel on the return trip. The 390th Bombardment Group (H) encountered as many as 100 hostile aircraft, both single and twin-engined fighters, attacking single, in pairs, and five abreast, simultaneously from all directions. The twin-engined fighters, screened by ME-109's and FW-190's, attacked with cannon and rocket projectiles. Fourteen enemy aircraft were destroyed and five additional were damaged. On this mission the 390th Bombardment Group (H) lost one of its own 15 aircraft while each of the other 14 aircraft were damaged. Antiaircraft fire ripped a hole in the windshield of the pilot's compartment, and put the automatic pilot out of commission, effectively preventing its use as an aid in the bombing run. The excellence of the bombing pattern, set under these difficult conditions, and the precision with which it was followed by the other aircraft of this unit, testify to the skill and gallantry displayed. All aircraft bombed the target. Of the 94,000 pounds of bombs dropped by this unit, 36,000 pounds landed within a 1,000-foot target area, and 79,000 pounds hit within a 2,000-foot area. It is conservatively estimated that it would take from 6 to 9 months for the enemy to restore the factory's normal rate of production, and the intervening lost production could never be made up. Despite the difficulties and dangers of the alerted enemy defenses this organization succeeded in attacking and seriously damaging a vital war industry. The aggressiveness, courage, heroic determination, and skill of the officers and enlisted men of the 390th Bombardment Group (H) on this occasion were largely responsible for the success of the mission with a minimum of loss. By the serious damage of the vital industrial plants at Schweinfurt, Germany, this unit rendered an invaluable contribution to the war effort of the United States.

By order of the Secretary of War

OFFICIAL;
>G. C. Marshall,
Chief of Staff

ROBERT H. DUNLOP,
>Brigadier General,
Acting The Adjutant General.

>FREDERICK S. DAIGER III
2d LT., Air Corps.
100th Bomb Gp (H) AAF

Owen D. Roane

Just back from Schweinfurt

Healy Campbell Stipe Jarvie

The air and ground crew of THEBIGASSBIRD II just after completing the Schweinfurt trip.

"Black Thursday" October 14, 1943

Left to right standing: Curtis Campbell, Cowboy Roane, Omar Gonzales, Arthur Stipe, Pete Cook, and Ray Tomb.

Second Row: Robert Stuart, Roger Stroble, Patrick Healy, James Jarvie, and Richard Detweiler.

Sitting: Woodie Woodward, George Kennedy, Ray Morton, and J.E. Baggett.

Fred Lehman is not in the picture because he was probably goofing off somewhere.

Owen D. Roane

RJUKAN

AFTER THE SCHWEINFURT MISSION, Campbell and the other short timers on our crew were restless and apprehensive about their chances to make it through the next two missions. They had vivid recollections about the bad ones on which we had prevailed, but Stipe said it would be better just to take what came. On the seventeenth of October, despite a blanket of clouds, we departed for a small city in Germany near Cologne named Duren for an attempt to drop bombs by radar. The designation of the effort was "Pathfinder" and the use of that method lessened the effect of both fighters and flak. We found that dropping chaff, called window by the British, almost completely nullified the flak accuracy and hampered fighter vectoring. Duren was at the juncture of several rail lines that gave fine reflections for the radar images to aim the bombs. Sadly the clouds were too dense to fly through and too high to fly over so we returned without mission sortie credit.

The next day we tried again for Duren but went into the overcast at 30,000 feet and had to return. However, we did fly over France so we were awarded credit for another sortie, number twenty-four for most men of our crew. Another positive event that day was that Major Veal met us at deplaning with a pair of shiny gold bars to replace the pickle I had become so accustomed to wearing. He also told me my request for first lieutenant was submitted while we were still airborne. Being pleased with the overall results of the day, we could appreciate the news that we were again alerted for another try at hitting Duren with the help of radar. We had grown fond of Duren in a survival sort of consideration, but we didn't actually make the flight until the twentieth. We managed to reach a point where the Pathfinder aircraft did a bombs away act at 30,000 feet and we followed suit. As we turned to go home,

Stroble said he hoped we hadn't worn out our welcome at Duren as he learned to think rather fondly of that place.

Well that was it for Stipe and Campbell who were already first lieutenants, and they never seemed reluctant to leave the crew before their pilot attained the same rank. The gunners had already been promoted to technical sergeants and saw no need to tarry either. One last time Healy said, "Boy am I hungry." Campbell completed his oration:

> Life is real! Life is earnest!
> And the grave is not its goal
> Dust thou art to dust returnest,
> Was not spoken of the soul.

Howard Bassett, who had been assigned to our crew as navigator since the Schweinfurt mission, asked me where Curtis got all that literary junk, and I asked him if he didn't know that we had been flying with a highly educated man. As a matter of fact our erstwhile bombardier was a renowned graduate of Princeton. Howard looked duly impressed so I never mentioned I was speaking of Princeton High School in Texas.

After debriefing we noted that no fighters nor flak of consequence had been encountered, so I presented the proposition that none of the fighting crewmen of "The Bigassbird II" would want to go out on just a whimper. We would probably be scheduled some notable missions in the forthcoming days, but none attempted to change their image. We spoke cheerio to them and, with welcomed replacements, we went back to making war on the Hun.

We had been flying with the same eight combat ready crews since the trip to Munster. Seventeen new crews had arrived on base but time and weather would not allow for group training. Starting on the twenty-second we hit the sky full bore. We flew formation training until we dreamed in groups. We flew one and sometimes two training flights until on the twenty-seventh of October, the Hundredth Group was again declared combat ready. I logged 18 hours and 50 minutes during those six days.

On the thirtieth of October, the Group was scheduled for a mission over the Rhur Valley, but weather prevented it. We flew three more hours with a bomb load and landed with the same. On the first of November, we had another hour and a half with the same scenario. By the third, when we finally had a go, everyone seemed to be ready.

On the mission, we set out for the submarine pens at Wilhelmshaven, Germany. We dropped our bombs by Pathfinder means with results unknown. We had no fighters, little flak and no losses. It was reported to us at debriefing that we had flown with more than five hundred and fifty bombers in the largest such gathering of exclusively U. S. type ever over Occupied Europe. Two days later we were in the sky headed for Gelsenkirchen, Germany to bomb a synthetic oil plant, but due to weather we arrived back at Thorpe Abbotts five and one half hours later with our bombs in the belly and one more mission under our belts. I celebrated my birthday the next day by getting to fly a new B-17G on a local test. Two days later we returned to our friends in Duren by Pathfinder, but we still did little damage to the town as it was reported our results were poor. Other than getting to participate in Milk Run missions for sortie count, I was not impressed with that new fangled invention called Pathfinder.

Since I was declared lead pilot I was blessed with a different front end crew. My co-pilot was Reginald Smith, bombardier Robert Peel and navigator "Bubbles" Payne. We had flown the last three missions together and were picked to fly Division lead with Colonel Harding to a place where we were intensely disliked,

Munster by designation. Before we reached enemy territory a recall was given. With a sigh of relief, we turned back for home without looking for a "Target of Opportunity." We landed with gas load and bomb load on one of the short runways. Colonel Harding helped me with the brakes without even having to be asked. He had some questions for the Air Exec when the smoke cleared. The day wasn't a complete loss as Major Veal met me with the shiny silver bars, even though the gold ones still looked new.

On November the sixteenth of 1943 we started another long trip to Norway as lead crew. We didn't know for sure what the nature of our trip was, but we were told that it would be one that could shorten the war if conducted successfully, or hurt our relations with Norway if a blunder were made. Remembering our previous trip to Trondheim, we knew we would see some beautiful scenery along the way.

As happened many times before, we would take off and climb immediately through the overcast in darkness before we could assemble our group into formation for the mission; however, this time we made it on top after climbing just three thousand feet. The long trip was made in relatively relaxed atmosphere for most of the crew, but radio operator Ray Tomb and engineer Robert Stuart were on their twenty-fifth mission. They seemed rather nervous as many warned that it was the jinxed sortie and they wanted this one to come off without a cold bath in the North Sea.

Riding with me was a new fellow with gold leaves and advanced age. His name was John M. Bennett of whom we were to learn much later on. The rest of the crew were the best to be had in the group. The navigator, Joseph H. "Bubbles" Payne, possessed skills that served us well on the trip. As we neared the Initial Point, we found clouds in the way. Our altitude was just twelve thousand feet and the mountains seemed to top out at nearly the same height. Payne noticed a crack in the clouds that would give a look at the target. We were somewhat early anyway so a circle and late turn could give us a west to east heading where the target could be seen. The powers that be didn't trust our radar bombing equipment enough to be used in friendly territory, so we had no "Pathfinder" aircraft.

Robert Peel, our bombardier, was beyond doubt the most effective bomb aimer in the group. He lived up to his reputation again as he very competently dropped the eggs on the target, as was evidenced by bomb impact photos viewed at the Third Air Division critique conducted at Elveden Hall. We had received an eighty-five percent score of hits in the inner circle of the target. We were taken to the wood shed though for bombing two minutes early and out of turn.

Major Bennett, soon to be our squadron commander and group commander, was flying his first mission with the Hundredth Group. He was flying as Air Boss in the co-pilot seat of Big Bird. Co-pilot, Reggie Smith, was flying in the tail gunner spot as observer and formation control officer. He was an experienced pilot just waiting to take over the crew whenever, if ever, I completed my tour. Reggie had recently transferred into our group from duty with the Royal Air Force. He had come over as a Flight Officer so, you see, I could empathize with him.

Robert Stuart completed his missions on that trip. He certainly did his job in outstanding manner as he had always done throughout the European tour. Also Ray Tomb completed his combat duty that day by sending a Strike Message declaring the target was accurately bombed and the group was returning.

We suffered one lost airplane that day. Pete Biddick was hit by flak and had to turn toward Scotland, where he crash-landed. On another day on another trip to Norway another pilot from the Hundredth lost his ship from crash landing in Scotland. His name was Curtis Biddick. I wondered if the Scots concluded that Biddick was another name for Yank.

At debriefing during the congratulations for Stuart and Tomb, Stu said he wasn't through until I was through. He had been a considerable part of our making it home from twenty-four trips. I hadn't gone to battle without him and Ray Tomb, but I assured them that we would be put on a "Milk Run" for my last flight. Anyway, I could recommend Dettweiler for the flight engineer position. That was the argument that I used to persuade them that the war must go onward without them. I don't remember seeing either of them again over on that side of the "Big Drink." None of the bunch that went over with us on the crew had been wounded nor did they need to face that prospect again in the future. I thanked the Lord for such a dedicated collection of men and for His protection until their final removal from "Harm's Way."

THE HEAVY WATER OPERATION

The following is a brief account of the action taken by the allies to deny the German war machine the use of Hitler's secret weapon as recorded in "Norway's Resistance Museum."

During the war, heavy water was considered indispensable as an aid to the production of atomic arms. The only plant in the world where heavy water was produced continuously was situated at Vemork (Rjukan) Norway. High priority was therefore given to the destruction of this plant.

GROUSE I supplied intelligence. GROUSE II prepared the landing area for two gliders carrying 34 British commando. Operation FRESHMAN, ended in catastrophe when the gliders crashed near the coast.

An operation, code-named GUNNERSIDE (6 men), joined GROUSE (3 men) and blew up the plant on February 27, 1943.

The heavy water plant was subsequently rebuilt, and was in full operation after only about 2 months.

On November 16, 1943, the power station and adjacent plant were destroyed by US bombers, putting an end to the production.

On February 22, 1944, the HYDRO ferry, carrying the remaining supplies of semi-finished heavy water was sunk on Lake Tennisjo, thus ending the battle for heavy water....

The following accounts of the mission were written by the front end crew of "THE BIGASSBIRD II":

95

Owen D. Roane

Command Pilot's Narrative for Mission of 16 November 1943:

Before briefing, we usually do not know the target for the bombing mission. However, since I was leading this one, I knew we were going to Rjukan, Norway, to bomb an electrolysis plant which was operated by the Germans to make high explosives. Because of the short days in late November and the long distance of the mission, we had to take off before daylight and climb through the low hanging clouds at four hundred feet and assemble on top. This is always a bit nerve racking as each plane carried six 1,000-pound high explosive bombs and full load of gasoline (2,800 gallons). This means that the airplane has a gross weight of 65,000 pounds, which is well above its designed maximum of 52,000 pounds. Even in broad daylight with perfect weather I would be nervous with this load. The success of our takeoff and climb through the overcast was due to no skill of my own, but to Lieutenant Owen D. (Cowboy) Roane from Valley View, Texas, my pilot.

After breaking out on top of the overcast, we found a half moon which brightened things up somewhat; we circled over our field at three thousand feet and collected the rest of the planes as they came up through the clouds. After assembling the group, we climbed to fourteen thousand feet and started out across the North Sea to Norway. Since fighter opposition was not anticipated, we did not fly combat wing formation but proceeded as individual groups. Many other groups could be seen on all sides headed in the same direction.

The trip across the North Sea was uneventful. Cowboy Roane is a top pilot. In spite of all this good luck, I was a bit nervous about lowering down to twelve thousand feet and going into Norway. Intelligence had told us that there would be no fighter opposition and no flak at the target; nevertheless, we would be at nine thousand feet above the ground as the target altitude was three thousand feet: dead ducks for flak.

The bleak rocks and crevices of Norway looked grim from nine thousand feet. There were no cities, railways or roads to use for checkpoints. Captain Joseph Payne did some remarkable navigation over this difficult country. As we approached the I.P. we could see that we were going to have trouble with the 95th Bomb Group which was just ahead of us and slightly lower. They were leaving condensation trails that made visibility difficult as well as leaving propwash for us to contend with. In spite of all these handicaps, Payne directed us straight to the target, and Captain Robert Peel dropped our bombs directly on the electrolysis plant. Bombing time was 11:43. The 95th Bomb Group passed over the target without seeing it in time to bomb, so they had to circle and make a second run. I believe that Joe Payne and Bob Peel are the best bombardier-navigator team in the 8th Air Force.

JOHN M. BENNETT
Major, Air Corps,
Command Pilot

Lead Pilot's Narrative for Mission of 16 November 1943:

We took off at 06:25 hours and climbed individually to twelve thousand feet to rendezvous over Splasher #6. There were only twelve ships, but one more joined us before we arrived at Spasher #4.

We were twelve minutes early at this point so we made a slow 360 degree turn and picked up six more ships, making a total of nineteen. Two of these were from other groups. One had an "A" on its tail and the other had an "O" to fly with our "D"s. Put together they spelled DOA.

We climbed to sixteen thousand feet trying to clear the overcast, but about midway we had to let down and go under. The altitude at this point was fourteen thousand feet. From then on the weather was good and we descended to twelve thousand feet. At this point we were joined by three B-24's. We reached the Norwegian coast twenty-two minutes ahead of schedule. To take up this time, we made a 360 degree turn and arrived at the target two minutes ahead of time at 11:43 hours. The bombing run was made with the target visible.

There was no combat wing formation; the groups went in individually. The only deviation was the high squadron led by Jack Swartout peeled off over the target, made a 360 degree turn and bombed in squadron formation.

It was necessary to climb to eighteen thousand feet on the return just before we reached the British coast, Cromer, to escape the overcast. The indicated airspeed was kept at 155 at all times and there were no excessive power settings. Navigation was particularly good.

OWEN D. ROANE
1st Lt., Air Corps,
Lead Pilot

Lead Navigator's Narrative of 16 November 1943:

The 100th Bombardment Group flew as a separate Unit or Task Force. The group left Louth one minute after the briefed time. The rendezvous, as such, continued until the middle of the North Sea as we left the English coast with eleven ships in the formation and bombed the target with twenty-four, including two B-24s. The briefed course to the Norwegian coast and to the I.P. was paralleled about twenty miles to the north. The Norwegian coast was reached eighteen minutes early and as the group was briefed to bomb at 11:45 hours, this time was lost by a circle and the target was bombed at 11:43 hours. The group encountered dangerous weather on the return, which was made to Cromer rather than Louth as briefed.

The bomb run was made on a heading of 80 degrees magnetic heading, and the target was destroyed (apparently) by the 100th Bomb Group at 11:43. The altitude was the briefed twelve thousand feet indicated (9700 feet true). The equipment functioned without failure in all respects. The location of the compass in many ships and the lack of free air temperature indicator for use by the navigator are minor difficulties the navigator should correct.

JOSEPH H. PAYNE
Captain, Air Corps,
Lead Navigator

Bombardier's Narrative for Mission of 16 November 1943:

The C-2 computer was used with the A.B.C. attachment.
Due to a change in the flight plan caused by early arrival, the turn at the I.P. was only approximately five degrees. The bomb bay doors were opened at this point and the A.F.C.E. was turned over to the bombardier from the pilot. Snow covered ground changed the aspect of the terrain but caused no serious affects on the bombing. Two groups preceded the 100th over the target but failed to bomb. These groups left propwash and persistent condensation trails, which later interfered with the run considerably.
The weather was clear at the target, but the surrounding area was covered with a 5/10 or more low stratus clouds.
Bomb impacts were seen, and confirmed, in the M.P.I. The buildings were seen to blow up.

ROBERT K. PEEL
Captain, Air Corps,
Lead Bombardier

Owen D. Roane

Remarks from the Third Air Division Commander:

Low clouds and icing conditions made the pre-dawn takeoff and assembly on the mission very difficult. It was necessary for assembly to take place long before daylight, between layers of the overcast or on top of the overcast. Weather conditions averaged five hundred feet ceilings at bases. In spite of these handicaps, most of the groups completed partial assembly and departed the coast on time, although a good many aircraft failed to occupy their assigned positions in the proper group formations and some even flew with another division. Also some aircraft from both the First and Second Divisions assembled with the Third Division formations.

While pre-dawn takeoffs in good weather are entirely feasible, it is believed that night takeoffs in bad weather should be limited to missions of most extreme military urgency. An appreciable percentage of combat efficiency will be lost due to failure to complete assemblies and to assemble in proper order or even with the proper formation. In addition, where such takeoffs require immediate climb with heavy load, through thick overcast in heavy icing conditions, the risk of losing entire formations should be considered.

It is felt that the difficult requirements on this mission make the successful navigation particularly commendable.

RUSSEL A. WILSON
Colonel, Air Corps,
Commanding

According to General John Bennett in a letter to me some twenty years later it had been disclosed that the plant we bombed at

Rjukan was making "heavy water" for German atomic bomb experiments. He also sent me a book entitled "Assault on Norway" that detailed the complete and final destruction of their product.

Owen D. Roane

The Heavy Water Plant in Ryukan, Norway

FINAL MISSION

I WAS CALLED TO THE SQUADRON commander's office on November sixteenth to have a talk with Lieutenant Colonel Veal who had just been promoted and was being transferred to the Thirteenth Combat Wing Headquarters for further duty. He explained to me that he had recommended me for captain, but the request had been returned. A new order had been received to the effect that promotion to captain could be made only after being in grade for three months as first lieutenant and being currently on combat status. He said that arrangements had been made for me to go to group operations after my twenty-fifth mission and work as a briefing officer. It was hoped that a pilot that had been through the tour would be an appropriate person to exhibit so others could see that the task was within the realm of possibility. It was agreed that the assignment would not be removing me from combat status. I would delay my return to the United States only until the eleventh of February. In the meantime I should go on down to group and get acquainted with my new job.

On the twenty-second of November, Lieutenant Colonel Kidd, the group operations officer, called the staff together and told us that a bombing mission to Berlin was scheduled for the next day. I said that I could complete my tour in style being a participant on the first mission to "Big B." Colonel Kidd said that he was not sending my crew there as it would be my last mission, maybe the hard way. I told him that I hadn't gotten where I was by picking missions. He looked at me and said I was welcome to go, but I should return to my quarters and say absolutely nothing about the destination. Needless to say, I was in agreement on that subject. I began to wonder if my mouth had not overloaded my judgment. I also wondered if Smitty and the rest of the crew would feel differently about my rashness, so silence was surely the best solution to that problem.

On the twenty-third the crews were briefed very early for the trip to Berlin. I didn't hear any real voices of reluctance toward the venture, so I confessed my sins about the matter. To my relief Smitty, Peel and Payne said they wouldn't miss it for anything. I had a new radio operator for the occasion and Dettweiler now was the flight engineer with technical sergeant rank to go with the position. They also took the briefed trip matter of factly, but Colonel Harding called the crews back to the briefing room and spoke to us about security violations. Truck drivers and ground crew members reported knowing where we were going even before the mission was canceled. I am sure none of the alerted crew members were the source of the information.

Some local flying kept us busy the next two days. We were called to the briefing room on the twenty-sixth for a return to the Paris vicinity. This would be my ninth sortie in that locality and we witnessed a definite lack of hospitality on each occasion. This would be even more trying than the others for me.

At briefing Major Rovegno, our group maintenance officer, had implored all pilots to keep their machines on the hard surfaces as it took several men and tractors to remove them from the mud. When he wished me good luck on number twenty-five, I smarted off by saying that when I returned I was going to dump it in the mud. Well, the day was filled with surprises. True to expectations there were lots of flak and fighters to greet us. Our group lost a plane piloted by George Ford who was on the first mission with his crew. At the same time I saw a very large hole appear in our right wing. Later I was presented with the nose of a twenty millimeter shell that had exploded in the main gas tank. Perhaps the tank being full prevented a secondary explosion that would probably have removed the wing. I always thought that the Lord was looking out for our crew for some reason, but it was especially evident that day.

The hole in the wing went all the way through leaving room for a small donkey to pass through. I trimmed the controls and kept sufficient speed to keep from stalling. Back over the base I experimented with stalling speeds enough to know what my landing speed should be. We were instructed to land on runway one-five in case of problems that could tie up traffic on the long one.

Final Damage

It is well we took that suggestion because runway two-eight, the long one, led to Billy Draper's barn, and it would shortly take a hit that day by another errant aircraft. Most people interested in this story know the incident referenced here. Smitty read out the speed for me and was standing by to help me with the brakes because this was a relatively short runway and we were landing hotter than usual. When three wheels settled down, we got on the brakes to no avail. As we were nearing the end, I thought the mud of Thorpe Abbotts would help to slow us down. I veered off and we did experience the desired effect. However, at the end of the roll, I saw both Colonel Harding and Major Rovegno striding out from the control tower for some unknown reason. After looking over the damage and realizing I had no hydraulic fluid left for brakes, they congratulated me and all was well.

Last night, the first of February 1995, while eating catfish with Pete Cook of the 349th Squadron Maintenance, I asked how they got the "Big Bird" out of the mud and he explained that the use of a Cleetrack was required. I apologized, somewhat belatedly, for not returning to help him and the ground crew remove the plane. He said they just hauled it over to the base depot as it was in need of major repair. The trusty plane did return to fly again until it finally made a raid on Berlin that fateful March the sixth when fifteen planes were lost from the Hundredth. I left the base the day before for a cruise on that wonderful ship, "Ile de France." The Bird went down that day with its pilot William Murray.

At the reunion in Myrtle Beach, in 1979, Reggie Smith presented me with a "metal" made from a scrap of the plane he found while flying it later. It meant more to me than several of the other official medals I possess.

CHEERIO

WE MOVED INTO THE WAAF (Women's Army Air Force) quarters, and things got much better for us. Not because there were any of the objects the quarters were named for, but construction was of a more advanced nature than the metal Quonset huts. Stipe and Campbell left for home without experiencing the luxury. It now was only a few hundred feet to our ablution facility; however, with winter approaching, we had trouble enough trying to keep reasonably warm. The coke we had access to for fuel in our heater was very hard to ignite. One member of our living quarters had an ingenious plan for fire starting. He had discovered nearby a barrel of asphalt without a sealed lid. He wound a portion around a stick and placed it in the stove among the coke particles to hurry the flame. Things went well until one day, thinking more is better, he overloaded the stove and a large glob rolled out the front while burning onto the concrete floor. Smoke drove us out into the weather and, after the smoke subsided, we found everything inside was coated with soot. After clean up, we used alternate means of starting our fires.

There were some unused bureaus in our place with several drawers made of pine. The back panel of the drawers made very fine kindling. Things went well until only the front panels of the drawers were left. The remains were dismantled and stored in another unused bureau until needed. Spring inventory showed one bureau missing from the list. When the supply officer was investigating, it was explained that the missing piece of furniture was probably in Switzerland as a recent crew ending up there was using it to store their class A uniforms in. I was never sure that the story was accepted as I saw the supply officer walking away talking to himself.

Owen D. Roane

I was hanging around camp just wasting my time,
Out of a job and not earning a dime,
When up steps a fellow and says I suppose
You're a Fort driver by the looks of your clothes.
Well he figured me right cause a good one I claimed
Did he happen to have a bad un to tame?
Well he says I got one, a bad one to buck
A 17E that we use as a truck.

The above ditty was sung to the tune of "Strawberry Roan."

To set the record straight, I was chosen to fly some Operations people to RAF Northolt in London. The time was December the tenth according to my old trusty Form Five. Don Bertholf volunteered to navigate the mission for me, and as there wasn't a spare pilot to fly right seat, bombardier Bob Peel took the job. The VIPs were all loaded with class A bearing, and without incident we soon were there. When ready to return, our number one engine starter wouldn't energize. There were no parts available at that station for our plane and, not being sure if we were at a field where we had no specific business, I decided we must have a go. The B-17E had been stripped of turrets and other combat equipment and, so I reasoned, it would be no heavier than a C-47. I explained this to the men with me to reassure them. Bob said, "Let's go," and Don selected another station amidship for the takeoff. Number one was feathered with two and three running fine. We started number four and set it a little more than compensation for drag in order to keep it straight on the runway. We started our roll and easily gained enough speed for takeoff. Starting our short climb to enough altitude to safely unfeather and start number one with windmilling, I asked Peel to ease the props back to 2100 rpm; however, we both noted that we were at 2100 rpm and had been since our approach to the field. So that is why we had such a quiet takeoff. With all four running again, Bertholf guided us back to Thorpe Abbotts. The flight is listed as a two hour local flight.

On the thirtieth of December the following "Press Release Story" was posted:

AN EIGHTH AAF BOMBER COMMAND STATION, England -- The Flying Fortress Laden Maiden is a crumpled wreck somewhere in Germany – only the Luftwaffe knows just where. Her crew went down with her, and they too are somewhere in Germany – safe in prison camp their friends at this base hope. But this story is concerned primarily with the airplane, the Laden Maiden, and the terrific job of destruction she accomplished against Hitler's Reich in the thirty missions, without a single abortion.

The Maiden was on duty in the ETO almost exactly six months. It was June 29, 1943, when William W. Veal, of New Rochell, New York, touched her wheels down on an English Airdrome after the flight across the ocean. Major Veal, then a squadron commander, flew the Maiden on his first combat mission before going on to become operations officer of a Combat Wing. He turned the Maiden over to the Cowboy.

Cowboy's real name was Owen D. Roane, from Valley View, Texas. He came into the ETO as a Flight Officer and when he got the Maiden he was a full-fledged first pilot. Cowboy took the Maiden all over Europe. One of his early missions is still a record for distance. He was in the formation which took off from England and bombed Trondheim, Norway – a distance so long that intelligence officers had to paste additional sheets onto their briefing room maps in order to show the crews where they were going. The Forts were in the air twelve hours that day – the longest operational flight B-17's have made so far. Another was Regensburg. That was the famed shuttle-raid to Africa, the day the American planes were under constant attack from hundreds of German fighters for two hours and ten minutes without even a break for lunch. Sixty B-17's were lost on that trip. That was really the big league.

Roane and the Maiden took part in the Schweinfurt raid – the second trip which cost the AAF another sixty bombers. They went to Bremen to Stuttgart – all the tough ones. Altogether, the Cowboy clicked off thirteen missions aboard the Laden Maiden. Six fighters were credited to her gunners and not one single abortion.

Then for eleven missions she was in the hands of Second Lieutenant Donald H. Moede of Lincoln, Nebraska, who used to be desk clerk at the Plains Hotel, Cheyenne, Wyoming.

Laden Maiden clicked off thirty combat missions. The thirty-first came on December the thirtieth of 1943, and the target was Ludwigshafen, Germany. The Maiden didn't come back this time. Her obituary was written in that familiar and succinct line with which newspaper readers are so familiar, "One of our aircraft is missing."

The mechanics and engineers who had been keeping the Maiden going all those months took it pretty hard. The big bomber was of special interest in their life. They had changed her engines, patched up flak holes, changed her tires and one time when one main landing gear collapsed after a landing, they darn near had to rebuild her. The left wing went on that time with new props. But right to the end, two of her original superchargers were functioning – something to brag about. The last flight of the Laden Maiden was made with pilot Marvin Leininger and co-pilot Albert Witmyer. Only the navigator, Leonard McChesney, and bombardier, Charles Compton, survived. They evaded and returned to Thorpe Abbotts April 17, 1944.

The following day another Press Release read:

AN EIGHTH AAF BOMBER STATION, England ---- Captain Henry M. Henington, a Flying Fortress pilot from Houston, Texas brought to a thrilling close his operational career in the European Theater of Air War by blasting a German armament factory in a Paris suburb, on New Years Eve. Henington had been to Paris, but this was his twenty-fifth combat mission and there wasn't enough flak in all of Occupied France to keep him from returning this time for a well deserved New Years Eve celebration.

The son of Mrs. L. S. Henington of Houston, Texas, the twenty-two year old Fortress pilot, who achieved that ripe old age on Christmas, is a former student at the University of Houston and in civilian life a metallurgist. His father, the late L. S. Henington was a well-known World War I Fighter Pilot.

Henington established himself as one of the top-flight pilots in the hard hitting Eighth Air Force when he flew the Regensburg shuttle from England to Africa with a pause for bombing Regensburg, Germany, on the way. When his ship "Horny" landed in Africa, there were only five rounds of ammunition left on board and members of the crew had shot down four enemy aircraft and damaged five others.

On September the third while engaged in a bombing mission to the outskirts of Paris, Pilot Henington's skill and courage saved the lives of his crew when their ship ditched in the English Channel after enemy fire had knocked out two engines before "Horny" could reach her destined target, the Renault Factory. Henington and his crew were picked up by a British "Walrus," a seaplane of the Air Sea Rescue Service, after they floated some three and a half hours in the cold water of the Channel. The rescue plane couldn't take off with their heavy load so they taxied back to England.

About a month later Captain Henington brought his ship "Horny II" back from a bombing raid on Bremen, Germany with an engine feathered and another smoking. After flak knocked out their number one and number four engines, the crew began to figure their time had come. Nazi Focke-Wulf fighters closed in on the crippled Fortress. But Henington dived the bomber four thousand feet through a swarm of German fighters, went into furious evasive action, leveled off and high-tailed her for home. When "Horny II" hit the runway the two remaining good engines quit cold on her --- out of gas. The ground crew had to have the ship towed to her dispersal site.

The same day another Press Release:

AN EIGHTH AAF BOMBER COMMAND STATION, England --- This is a report to the good people anywhere in America, but it's particularly for the boys and girls of Fillmore high School, Fillmore, California. They'll want to know about their greatest school hero, Captain Walter U. Moreno and the nine other men who make up his crew, and especially about his Flying Fortress, Messie Bessie; because the youngsters in Fillmore High School named Messie Bessie and helped pay for her.

Captain Moreno and his crew have won their biggest game. They have completed their operational tour with the Eighth Air Force. That means that twenty-five times they have taken off from this concealed base in England, pointed across the Channel or the North Sea, battled their way across Europe and dropped their bombs squarely on another German war target. Those twenty-five missions included the longest to Trondheim, Norway, and the famous shuttle raid to Africa, when "Messie Bessie" hit the Messerschmitt factory at Regensburg on the way in and aircraft shops at Bordeaux, France on the way back. Captain Moreno and the officers and men of his crew are finished with this part of the war. Some of them hope to go back to the United States for awhile before going into some other theater of action. But "Messie Bessie" is still here and has great plans for the future. She'll pick up another great crew and start back again on the star routes over

Germany, each time with explosives to be dropped where they will do the most good to shorten the war and bring back the forces to their own United States. And the students of Fillmore High have had a big hand in doing all this.

On January first, 1944 Jack Justice returned to the base from a land tour of Western Europe to say goodbye and pick up captain bars. Henington had just finished along with Moreno the day before and all had their tracks in place to head back to the "Land of the Free." But the fourth member of the first replacement pilots, although he had finished the required twenty-five missions, was in waiting for the promotion that spelled a job completed. That fourth pilot having done twenty-five before the others was myself, now working in 349th Squadron Operations. Major Bennett had taken over as commander of the squadron and announced that anyone on combat status could expect to fly combat missions. So there you have it. I did fly additional missions. The last mission was flown on February twenty-ninth, 1944. I remember very little of that mission. Jim Brown's book is somewhat limited on the details. Red Bowman of Group Intelligence reports: "Off at 0730 for Brunswick. Returned at 1330, all safe. Russell Flack came in with two engines out from flak. Bombed by Pathfinder through 10/10. Saw no enemy fighters, but friendly fighters were thick as bees." I don't remember whom I flew with that day but I logged four hours of combat time.

The 349th daily Journal of March 1, 1944 read: Mo (originally named Mohammed, regardless of her gender) died today, despite efforts of amateur veterinarians in the Squadron, and a professional summoned from a nearby town. Her fatal illness was not definitely diagnosed; she was stricken only about twenty-four hours before her death, with symptoms of great pain and rasping breath. Some thought it was pneumonia while others suspected that her omnivorous appetite, which caused her to devour soap, sticks and cinders as voraciously as she did candy, chewing gum and cookies, may have brought her to her doom, through the ingestion of some poisonous or congestive substance.

Mo had lived harmoniously and amusingly with the Squadron since August 1943, when she was flown back from North Africa by Cowboy Roane's crew, returning from the famous Regensburg shuttle raid. On her ride from her native sands to the green pastures of East Anglia, Mo was posted in the radio room with Ray Tomb. She wore a sheepskin jacket and wore an oxygen mask. This was not the first account of a jackass in sheep's clothing, but she earned credit for a combat mission since her plane bombed Bordeaux, France on the return trip. Mo weighed about twenty-five pounds, and was supposed to have been some six months old when she joined us. Her weight had increased to perhaps eighty pounds at the time of her death. She was highly intelligent, gentle and sociable in appearance; she was as delightfully comic as a Disney creation. Her passing left a distinct void in the Squadron's life, and there were some who linked the loss of our mascot and the departure of pilot, Cowboy Roane, on the fifth of March with the grievous luck of our combat on the sixth of March. Mo was given a quiet but fitting burial in the Squadron area, and her grave was appropriately marked. "There is some corner of a foreign land that is forever Algeria."

No Mo

Continuing the Journal of March 4, 1944: "Cowboy (Owen D.) Roane left for the states today, wearing well deserved Captain's bars. The diminutive Texan had proved in twenty-seven missions to be one of the ablest, most calmly fearless and daring of all our great pilots; and his personality endeared him to all of us who came in contact with him, from KP's to Colonel."

On March sixth, 1944, the first day of my long journey home, I was thinking that this was the first birthday anniversary of my brother, Orville, since the B-26 crash that took his life last March fifteenth. I never knew that it would be the day that fifteen crews of the Hundredth Bomb Group would not be returning. My plane, "The BIGASSBIRD II," was among the many to be lost. I never knew of this disaster that once again nearly wiped out all my friends, a second time, until I read James Brown's book in 1988. As the English say, "Cheerio."

A Cowboy's trips over Europe

04 July 1943	La Pallice
10 July 1943	Le Bourget
14 July 1943	Le Bourget
17 July 1943	Hamburg
24 July 1943	Trondheim
25 July 1943	Warnemunde & Kiel
26 July 1943	Hanover
29 July 1943	Warnemunde
12 August 1943	Wesseling
15 August 1943	Merville & Lille
17 August 1943	Regensburg
24 August 1943	Bordeaux-Merignac
31 August 1943	Meulan LesMeureaux
02 September 1943	Kerlin-Bastard
03 September 1943	Paris & Beaumont
06 September 1943	Stuttgart
07 September 1943	Watten
09 September 1943	Beauvais-Tille
08 October 1943	Bremen
14 October 1943	Schweinfurt
18 October 1943	Duren
20 October 1943	Duren
03 November 1943	Wilhemshaven
05 November 1943	Gilsenkirchen
07 November 1943	Duren
16 November 1943	Rjukan, Norway
26 November 1943	Paris
29 February 1943	Brunswick

EPILOGUE

OF THE MANY MEMBERS of the 100th Bombardment Group in England during my tour of duty, too much is unknown. Of those I was most closely associated with, I will attempt to close their chapters. Anyone reading this delayed journal having further information about the individuals I have written about are requested to furnish this information to me so I can complete this record. I am closing this writing only temporarily as of the ninth of September 1995, fifty-two years after my eighteenth mission.

Co-pilot Arthur C. Stipe went home in October of 1943, having been the second pilot to have completed twenty-five missions. Our trails crossed again in November of 1944 when I was assigned to the Seventh Ferry Group at Great Falls, Montana where he was the assistant operations officer. He helped Betty and I get an apartment in the place where he lived. He further gave me orders to Homestead, Florida to check out on the C-54 transport aircraft. He is currently living in Bend, Oregon, having retired from the forest fire fighting business. I got to meet with Bud and Lou Stipe again on the eighth and ninth of June at Walla Walla, Washington for the commemorative program designating the base there as a principal training base for bomber crews going overseas in 1943. It was at Walla Walla that I first met Bud. They are planning to attend the "Black Thursday" reunion in San Antonio on the fourteenth of October 1995, to commemorate the fifty-second anniversary of the second mission to Schweinfurt. We will meet again there. I hope Navigator Gonzales and Bombardier Campbell will also be there.

Bombardier Curtis K. Campbell also went home in October of 1943 minus fifty pounds net weight and with much more intelligence. In fact the next time I saw him was in June of 1944 at the Ardmore, Oklahoma Air Base serving as intelligence officer. Our paths have crossed numerous times since. Betty and I shared his life with his family on many occasions, and also his grief in the passing of his wife Lois. He is currently living in Lewisville, Texas just thirty-five miles away. We see him often.

Navigator Daniel L. Schmucker stayed with the Air Force and was involved as a pioneer with radar navigation and bombing. He retired from the Air Force in the rank of colonel, but died some years ago in his beloved New Orleans.

Engineer Robert A. Stuart returned to the United States in December of 1943 to become engineer on "The Magic Carpet," Lieutenant General Knowland's plane, when he was commanding the Air Transport Command. I met with Stuart in Honolulu, Hawaii and Frankfort, Germany during service. In 1973 Betty and I went by Rantoul, Illinois for a short visit with him and his wife Wanda before riding with them to Milwaukee, Wisconsin to attend the Hundredth Reunion there. Red Stuart died a few months later.

Ball Turret Gunner Roger O. Stoble went home from England in October of 1943 and I lost track of him until the 1973 reunion in Milwaukee where Betty and I had a visit with him and his wife Mildred. He also died shortly after the reunion.

Radio Operator Clarence R. Tomb was out of touch until the reunion in San Antonio, Texas, in 1979. There we became reacquainted. We have become good friends again, and we hope to visit with him in Fort Worth, Texas in October of this year. He and his wife Hazel live in Lititz, Pennsylvania.

Gunners Patrick J. Healy and James Jarvie also finished their tour in October to return to Philadelphia, Pennsylvania, where no positive word has been heard of them since.

Co-pilot Reginald Smith who flew in the tail gunner's position as group formation coordination officer on the Rjukan, Norway raid and later became pilot of the crew, was shot down over Denmark in February of 1944. He was taken prisoner by the German Occupation Army, released by the Russians toward the end of the war and returned home. I had the opportunity to visit with him at both Milwaukee and the 1982 Myrtle Beach reunions before his death in 1984.

Lead Navigator Joseph H. Payne who flew with me on the last five missions of my regular tour, was killed on a mission in April after I left for the United States in March of 1944.

Bombardier Robert Peel had to bail out of a burning airplane in March of 1944 just ten days after I left for home. He was a prisoner until after the war was over. I never had the opportunity to visit with him again before he died in 1952.

Group Command Pilot John M. Bennett gained the rank of Major General before his military career was finished. I had the pleasure of visiting with him through the years and he always reminded me of the significance of the raid on the heavy water plant in Norway. He died on his ranch in Texas in May of 1993. He requested his ashes be returned to Thorpe Abbotts.

Jack Justice had a near parallel career with my own at many points. We trained at Walla Walla, Washington together, went overseas at the same time and were both assigned to the 100th Bombardment Group as their first replacements. We both came home with Captain's bars in early 1944 and we trained for the Berlin Airlift together at Great Falls, Montana and we went over again on the same orders. We both retired from the Air Force as lieutenant colonels. On Memorial Day of this year, 1995, I received word of the death of Jack. I went to Riverside, California, for his burial in the National Cemetery there.

Crew Chief Ray Morton returned home after the war to married Thelma (a name that appeared on the airplane I flew to England) and had a career as part owner and general manager of the Pascot Floor Management Company in Seattle, Washington. We met again at the Long Beach reunion in 1987 and Ray and Thelma hosted me at Seattle on my stop over before going back to Walla Walla this year. We have enjoyed our renewed friendship over the last many years.

Ray Morton presented Legion of Merit
by General Partridge

Henry M. Henington finished his twenty-five missions in early 1944 and also made a career of the Air Force. The last time I saw him was in Rapid City, South Dakota. He was with General Henry Sullivan and had made Colonel prior to retirement. I heard he was killed some years ago while flying a fire fighting plane in the western United States.

Walter Moreno finished his tour in early 1944 and returned to the United States. I haven't heard anything of him since.

Colonel Neil Harding was Deputy Commander Pacific Air Force in 1948 when I was assigned to Guam with Military Air Transport Service (MATS). I had the opportunity to visit with him at Hickam Field. He made General but died shortly thereafter. I thought he was the greatest commander of all.

Jack (John) Herlihy who did such an outstanding job as maintenance officer is doing an equally fine job with the Hundredth Bomb Group Association in any and all tasks. He is one of the main reasons that the association is progressing with such great success.

Aircraft Inspector Pete Cook is back in Saint Jo, Texas, where he has had a wonderful ranching career. He and his wife and Betty and I get together periodically to eat and discuss old times.

Sam Barr is no longer with us. We visited in San Antonio at the reunion in 1979. I read of his death in Splasher Six in 1986.

Sumner Reeder of "Squawkin Hawk" fame preceded me to Homestead, Florida to fly the C-54, but by the time I arrived he was missing from a flight over the Gulf of Mexico. That was in June of 1945.

Group Orientations Officer Jack Kidd was still with the group when I left to return to the United States. I never heard of him again until I was in Frankfurt, Germany, doing my duty with the Berlin Airlift. I hear he had a career with the Air Force and retired as a Major General. He is planning to attend the 1995 reunion at Ft. Worth.

Squadron Commander William Veal is one of those people that has been hard for me to find. I owe him so very much for my successful tour in England. He showed confidence in me and was always around to give words of encouragement and to tell me that I was losing my hair. Little I knew at the time that what he was telling me was true. I note it whenever I shave. I just located him in Washington State last Friday, August 31, 1995, in time to send him a copy of this book.

Glenn Dye was the first pilot to complete twenty-five sorties with the 100th Bomb Group. His was the only original crew to complete a tour out of the European Theater still generally intact. A few other pilots did do the assigned number of missions as individuals. After the war Glenn formed and operated a flying school and charter service in Ohio. At the Long Beach Reunion I was able to spend much time with him and his son, for whom he named his planes "Sunny" and Sunny II." He died in January of 1988.

Howard Bassett who flew three missions with us as Navigator is currently living in Illinois. I have tried to pick his brain about the trips he took with our crew but, sadly, he can't fill in many of the blanks.

Robert Hughes, who led half of our eight planes to Schweinfurt by tagging on to the 95th Bombardment Group, arrived at our base on the fourteenth of July 1943. He was one of the second four replacement crews. If my memory serves me right, all four completed their assigned tour of combat. His service career closely parallels my own. He retired from the Air Force as Lieutenant Colonel and now lives in Wenatchee, Washington. I had the privilege of visiting with him and Elaine in Walla Walla while there this year.

Cowboy Roane, that's me, retired from the Air Force in 1963 as a Lieutenant Colonel. Shortly after the Air Lift I was caught in the Reduction In Force (RIF) as far as pilot status was concerned. I went to Keesler Field to become an Electronics Countermeasures Observer to regain flying pay. I felt that I had been treated badly by the RIF because I had given up a perfectly good job punching cattle in 1948 for a recall to fly MATS in the Pacific. Since I found I liked the Electronics Intelligence field, I turned down restoration to pilot assignment for the Korean War. In fact the rest of my career was in ELINT. Afterwards I spent twenty-three more years in public education, which is a war that has yet to be drawn to a successful conclusion. I look forward to all reunions as the people I get to visit with there played such a large part in the most significant era of my life.

Owen D. Roane

Valley View, Texas
Memorial Day, 1995

John K. Justice

Dear Old Friend,

Yesterday I heard the report that you were again missing from the formation. It saddened me greatly, but not so much as when I heard the report of your missing in action on the tenth of October 1943. This time I will not be worried about your future. On this Memorial Day the memories come flooding back, and how great they are.

It was in March of 1943 that I met you and liked you immediately. It was in Walla Walla, Washington, where we were both in training as pilots of combat air crews. It is so appropriate that I come by California on my way to join in commemoration of the old air base. I will be a representative of our dear 100th Bombardment Group. It was mean of me when we finally started our trip across to cause you to have to fly the Big Boss over to England as an unwelcome addition to your crew.

When I persuaded you to go with me back to the 100th Bombardment Group to fly our combat tour, I didn't have any warning about what we were getting into. I flew by the side of you on your first mission, which was to Kiel, Germany. That certainly was a baptism by fire. We were together on the Regensburg - Bordeaux shuttle where only five of twenty-one of our group made the round trip successfully. We were together on the third of September when my original pilot, King, and our close friend Henington went down with four others of our group. Three days later on the mission to Stuttgart you saw me leave the formation on fire and going down. You shared your joy when the Lord's mighty hand saw me safely home. I went to the hospital and worried about you and my crew for a month.

I returned on October the eighth to fly with you to Bremen, Germany, where eight of our planes failed to return. I didn't go on the next trip to Munster, Germany, just two days later when you failed to return to the base. I thought our friendship had come to an end, but thanks to the Lord, we would have many years yet. When you did return from walking out of Europe, I was happy in turn. We both went our own ways and supposed again that our time together had ended.

We were recalled to the service in 1948 to train in Great Falls, Montana for flying the Berlin Airlift, and as fate would have it we were sent to Germany on the same orders. We both stayed in the Air Force until retirement and went our own way until the group reunion at Dayton, Ohio in

1985. I was looking forward to meeting again this year as we had so often done in past reunions.

I have just received the report that you are again missing from the formation and will not rejoin us. You did a wonderful job while you were with us. I never told you that I thought you were the greatest of the bunch, but that will be taken care of when we meet again. I know you are having a wonderful life at your new station and enjoying the peace you so richly deserve. I would imagine you are again flying the Boss around. I will miss you sorely.

Your friend forever,

Cowboy Roane

P. S.: Tell the Boss to save a place on the flight roster for me.

SCALING THE ALPS

Four B-17s fly over the Alps enroute to Africa. Henington's plane Horny, Roane's plane Laden Maiden, Wolff's plane Wolf Pack and the lower B-17 is "Bucky" Egan and "Crankshaft" Cruikshank in Mugwump.

The following article was written by Mike Faley after the 100th Bomb Group reunion in Salt Lake City, Utah in 1998. Published in the Splasher Six, Volume 29, Fall 1998, No. 3. Reprinted by permission from its author.

The Last Cowboy

As five stately gentlemen stand in the lobby of a Salt Lake City Hotel reminiscing about their youthful exploits, Brian hesitantly approaches the group.

Being a member of the 918th Bomb Group re-enactors, (invited to Salt Lake to display their massive collection of 8th Air Force memorabilia at the 100th Bomb Group reunion), he asks this author to introduce him to these war wary veterans. When I introduce him to **Owen Roane**, he steps back, eyes wide, speechless, and in awe. Pulling me aside he asks, is that "The Cowboy"?

One of seven brothers to serve in World War II, Pilot Owen Roane, would begin his exploits in the ETO on June 26, 1943. A Second Lieutenant, Owen Roane (upon his own request!) is assigned to the 100th BG (H) at Thorpe Abbotts. Due to the loss of three aircraft and crews on the previous day's mission to Bremen, Owen is assigned to the 349th Squadron, under the command of Captain **William Veal**. The Group had not yet received its notorious moniker of the "Bloody Hundredth" but this first mission was an ominous foreboding of events to come. Assigned to Captain Veal's plane "Laden Maiden" Owen and crew would complete 10 rugged missions before engaging in one of the fiercest air battles of WWII.

On the morning of August 17, 1943 the 100th BG was given the unenviable task of being low and last group on the mission to bomb the ME 109 factory at Regensburg. Being in the "Coffin Corner" left the 100th and Owen the most vulnerable to the

Luftwaffe and nine planes of the group were lost that day. (A total of 60 B-17s were lost on the Schweinfurt/Regensburg mission). Even though Owen always felt this inner sense that he would complete his tour of duty, the events of this day would "serve as a warning that we all faced death on each and every mission we flew." One such example was the crew of Lt. **Henry Shotland** who was flying in *"The WAAC Hunter"* (second element of the high squadron). Shotland and his crew were roommates with Owen and this was their first mission. It would also prove to be their last. Jumped by three fighters and with the left wing ablaze, everyone bailed out (except the tail gunner who went down with the plane) and become POWs.

The other vivid memory of this battle, indelibly etched in Owen's mind, was the plight of Lt. **Curtis Biddick** and his crew. Flying *"Escape Kit"* in the second element, lead squadron, Biddick's plane suffered an oxygen fire caused by 20mm damage to the nose and fuselage, trapping those on the flight deck. With flames raging through the nose and cockpit, the co-pilot, **Richard Snyder**, climbed out onto the wing, reached back into the flaming B-17 to retrieve his parachute and slid off the wing. As Snyder's chute opened, he was immediately propelled into the horizontal stabilizer of *"Escape Kit"*, and his chute became entangled on it. According to reports, Snyder was seen trapped on the stabilizer as the plane went down. Four from Biddick's crew were KIA (including Biddick and Snyder).

Cowboy, flying *"Laden Maiden"* in the number 2 position, high squadron, would watch the ragged remains of the 100th limp across the Alps and onward toward North Africa. To his left he could see the damaged aircraft of **Bob Wolff** flying in the lead element with a huge section of his horizontal stabilizer badly in need of repair. It would not be until landing at Telergma that the extent of damage to his own aircraft would be known. The *"Maiden"* had been peppered with 212 bullet and flak holes.

It would be upon the 100th's return from North Africa on August 24, 1943 that Owen would provide an immense sense of humor for a group much in need and a mascot as well. It seems that the crew decided to bring back a living souvenir from North Africa, a donkey named "Mo". An oxygen mask was hooked up in the radio room for Mo, and upon returning to Thorpe Abbotts (Station 139) red flares were fired signaling medical help was needed. The Control Tower asked what the problem was. Owen replied, "I'm coming in with a frozen ass." When the doctor arrived at the plane, he was astonished to find a real jackass.

Cowboy Roane would go on to distinction participating in such other great Air Battles as Bremen, October 8, 1943 ("the most accurate flak that I've ever seen in my life") and Schweinfurt – "Black Thursday" October 14, 1943, but it would be on a relative unknown mission to Rjukan, Norway on November 16, 1943 that would really affect the outcome of the war effort. Although not briefed on the extreme importance of the mission, the target that day was the Heavy Water plant instrumental to Germany's effort to develop atomic weapons. Leading the 100th Bomb Group, recently promoted Lt. Roane, along with Command Pilot Major **John Bennett**, flew in "*The Bigassbird II*" with Group Navigator **Joseph "Bubbles" Payne** and "**Dead Eye**" Bombardier **Robert Peel**. Cowboy and company found the target through a hole in the cloud cover, courtesy of "Bubbles", and dropped their bombs right on target. A mission critique would verify that the 100th BG hit the target with 85% of their bombs in the target although the only flak they received was for bombing out of turn. The damage inflicted upon the Heavy Water plant stopped Germany's production of heavy water and deprived their scientists of the ability to develop atomic weapons. On his final mission to Paris, Cowboy made a joke to the group maintenance officer that he was going to dump his plane in the soft Thorpe Abbotts mud upon his return. Over the target a 20mm hole big enough to fit a body through ripped up the right wing, and Owen had to nurse the plane back home only to see the "*Bigassbird II*" turn his joke into reality, with the right wing off the end of the runway into the mud as promised. Both the CO and the group maintenance officer held up short of reading Owen the riot act once they saw the condition of the aircraft.

That mission and illustrious landing earned him entrance into the "Lucky Bastard Club" (entrance is contingent upon completing 25 missions), Captain's Bars, and a trip back to the States on March 6, 1944 (date ring a bell – Big "B"). Cowboy retired from the Air Force a Lt. Colonel in 1963 and lives in Valley View, Texas with his wife Betty. By the way, the nickname "Cowboy" was given to Owen after a Staff Sgt. inquired about his profession before enlisting. Naturally, when Owen said he was a cowboy, the name stuck.

…After nodding my head yes, that is "Cowboy Roane," Brian joins our circle to hear the tales of a time when 19 year old cowboys rode their Warbirds against overwhelming odds. They were never turned back and many perished to preserve future generations. I always thought of a cowboy as a symbol of the American drive, determination, sense of fair play and pure resolve to overcome any hardship or take on any challenge. Owen Roane is all that and more, a true gentleman, a leader, and one of the legends of the "Bloody Hundredth". His kind of cowboy may never be seen again.

TAPS

O wen D. "Cowboy" Roane passed away January 2, 2002 at his ranch in Valley View, Texas, surrounded by his family. He put up a gallant fight against cancer and left us as he lived, with dignity, pride and courage. Owen was born November 6, 1921, one of nine boys. During the war he was a pilot with the 349th Squadron. He led the raid on the heavy water plant at Rjukin, Norway, and went on to complete 28 missions from July 4, 1943 to February 29, 1944. From his first mission to his last, Owen's gentle manner never changed, nor did his wit. Red Bowman, of Group Intelligence, reported in his journal of March 5, 1944, "Cowboy (Owen D.) Roane left for the states today, wearing well-deserved Captain's bars. The diminutive Texas had proven in twenty-seven missions to be one of the ablest, most calmly fearless and daring of all our great pilots; his personality endeared him to all who came in contact with him, from KP's to Colonels." Anyone who knew him would agree that was Owen.

Owen will be forever remembered for his exploits, his dry humor, his leadership abilities and his service to the 100th Bomb Group both during the war and afterwards, with the Association and later the Foundation. Owen was a "true legend," someone this Group could count on and lean on. He was soft spoken and mild mannered but decisive. He could always assess a difficult situation and come up with a logical answer. As President of the Association from 1991 through 1993, Cowboy helped to nurture young members for the Group's future. It was through these efforts that Paul West and the rest of the Historical Staff were encouraged to join the Association/Foundation. He was a great inspiration to everyone he met, but to the historical staff, he was a mentor, and more importantly, a friend.

Owen, a highly decorated combat pilot, retired from the Air Force in 1963, and for the next twenty years spent his time in education and public service. Married for over 58 years, Owen is survived by the love of his life, Betty, and their four children: son John and his wife Gail; daughter Martha and her husband Randy;

Owen D. Roane

son Tom and his wife Cherilyn; daughter Carol; as well as eight grandchildren and two great grandchildren. He is preceded in death by his parents and eight brothers. Owen was buried on January 5, 2002 in his Air Force uniform with full military honors in the company of family, friends, and twenty members of the 100th Bomb Group. To Owen "Cowboy" Roane we say, "Thank you, our dear friend, for your courage, your honor, and most of all, your service and friendship." Owen Roane was "The Last Cowboy" of his kind, we will not see another like him in our lifetime. Goodbye, our friend.

Mike Faley, Jan Riddling, Cindy Goodman

Reprinted with permission from *Splasher Six*, Volume 32, Winter 2001, No. 4.

Epilogue Addendum

Since Owen closed his writing in September 1995, there is further word of some of those mentioned in the Epilogue.

He received a call from Henry Henington assuring him that he was alive and well. It was a red-letter day for Owen then, and another when Henry and Katherine came to see him February 17, 2001. They live in Air Force Village in San Antonio, Texas.

He was saddened to learn of the loss of his friend, Jack Herlihy on November 3, 2000 and of three of his crew members: Curtis Campbell on September 4, 1997, Clarence Tomb on March 6, 2000, and Pete Cook on October 25, 2001.

The 100th has suffered many losses through the war years and since. The Roane family felt the heartache that many families have felt when they lost Owen on January 2, 2002.

"Cowboy" & Betty Roane

ACKNOWLEDGEMENTS

I would like to thank those who have had a part in the reprinting of Owen's book.

My family encouraged me to pursue my desire to reprint his book as a tribute to Owen's memory. Martha's husband, Randy Reedy, and his friends, Julie Singletary and Curt Batson, were primarily responsible for editing and publishing this reprinted version.

The 100th Bomb Group Foundation Historical Staff - Mike Faley, Jan Riddling, Cindy Goodman, and Greg Hatzenbuhler – were supportive, as always, advising and assisting in numerous ways. The Foundation website was a great source of information, thanks to Webmasters Charlie Cole, Harry Nelson, and Paul West.

Many members have served through the years to support the Foundation. English friends had a vision which led to the founding of the Memorial Museum at Thorpe Abbotts.

I would like to add my appreciation for their dedication to the preservation of the heritage of the 100th Bomb Group.

Betty Roane

Owen D. Roane

IN MEMORY OF

MIKE HARVEY

FOUNDER

CPSIA information can be obtained at www.ICGtesting.com
Printed in the USA
LVOW10s2037160713

343163LV00001B/235/A